REMEMBER

Stories and poems for self-help and self-development based on techniques of Ericksonian and auto-hypnosis

Gary Edward Gedall

16/03/2011

I

Published by

From Words to Worlds,

Lausanne, Switzerland

www.fromwordstoworlds.com

Deposited in the Bibliothèque nationale Suisse April. 2014, under the title of 'REMEMBER - Stories and poems for self-help and self-development based on techniques of Ericksonian and auto-hypnosis ', written by Gary Edward Gedall.

Cover by: Pierre Weyrich   www.pietw.com
Cover image, "**No man's land**", oil on canvas
by Daniel Will - www.danielwill.ch .
Edited by Prof J. J. Gordon   jj.gordon@bluewin.ch

ISBN: **2-940535-11-8**
ISBN 13: **978-2-940535-11-8**

By the same Author

Adventures with the Master

Tasty Bites
(Series – published or in preproduction)
Face to Face
Free 2 Luv
Heresy
Love you to death
Master of all Masters
Pandora's Box
Shame of a family
The Noble Princess
The Ugly Barren Fruit Tree
The Woman of my Dreams

The Island of Serenity, Pt 1 Destruction
(Series – published or in preproduction)

Book1 :	**The Island of Survival**
Book 2:	**Sun & Rain**
Book 3:	**The Island of Pleasure (Vol 1)**
Book 4:	**The Island of Pleasure (Vol 2)**
Book 5:	**Rise & Fall**
Book 6:	**The Island of Esteem**
Book 7:	**The Faron Show**
Book 8:	**The Island of Love**

(Non Fiction)   **The Zen approach to Low Impact Training and Sports**

About the Author

Gary Edward Gedall is a state registered psychologist, psychotherapist, trained in Ericksonian hypnosis and EMDR.

He has ordinary and master's degrees in Psychology from the Universities of Geneva and Lausanne and an Honours Degree in Management Sciences from Aston University in the UK.

He has lived as an associate member of the Findhorn Spiritual Community, has been a regular visitor to the Osho meditation centre in Puna, India. And as part of his continuing quest into alternative beliefs and healing practices, he completed the three-year practical training, given by the Foundation for Shamanic Studies in 2012.

He is now, (2014 – 2016), studying for a DAS, (Diploma of Advanced Studies), as a therapist using horses.

Quora writer of the year 2015

His hobbies are; writing, western riding and spoiling his children.

He is currently living and working in Lausanne, Switzerland.

Acknowledgements

First and foremost, I would like to thank my wife, Dr Mona Cserveny Gedall, who drew me over to Switzerland and suggested that I might enjoy psychology as a profession. Who also suggested that I include the clinical vignettes in the book.

To my children who have demanded and continue to demand that I make up stories for them.

To all my teachers over the years but especially to Dr Gerard Salem, who took me in while still an undergraduate student taught me hypnosis and launched me on the track of becoming a working psychologist.

Finally, and maybe most importantly, to my patients, who have inspired me, these many years, to create and refine the stories and hypnotic inductions that you have before you.

Thank you

Gary Edward Gedall

5th April 2011, Lausanne, Switzerland

Contents

Part 1:   The Stories and Poems

Part 2:   A theoretical framework

Dusk falls, the world shrinks little by little into a smaller and smaller circle as the light continues to diminish.

The centre of this world is illuminated by a small candle, crystal, cauldron, crucifix, kris, column, cloud of smoking incense. The eager faces of the people gathered there are lit by the fire of their expectations.

The master, priest, teacher, therapist, group leader, shaman, witch doctor, medicine man (or their female counterparts), will begin to speak, they will explain to them how the world is, how it was, how it was created. They will help them understand how things have a sense, an order, a way that they need to be.

They will demonstrate how they should live, live together, live in harmony with themselves and with the visible and invisible worlds that contain them and are contained within them.

They will clarify the sources of un-wellness and unhappiness, what is sickness, where it comes from, how to notice it and… how to heal it.

To heal the sick, they will call forth the forces of the invisible realms, maybe they will sing, certainly they will talk, and talk, and talk.

The congregation will be moved by the words, energies will move within them, emotions will excite or calm their souls. At some point they focus towards the inner experiences which are much stronger and more interesting than the outer…the healing process has begun…

Since the beginning of time we have gathered round those who can bring us the answers to our questions and the means to alleviate our sufferings.

Sandra Ingerman, in her 'Author's note', introducing her book, on Soul Retrieval, reflects that 'Shamans have always been the healers and psychologists of their communities.
In all shamanic traditions the concept of telling healing words and healing stories… is prevalent.'

This practice has not fundamentally changed since the earliest times; in every era, continent and culture we have found and continue to find these experiences.

This book is dedicated to all the teachers and healers who have given, who give and who will give, so much of themselves in the service of others

Self-development and self-help using these stories and poems

The stories and poems that you will find below have been created and later expanded and re-written with the intention that the reader would find a therapeutic benefit but also, and just as importantly, that the experience of listening to or reading them should be a pleasant experience.

The messages that they contain, which are many and on multiple levels – as with other 'motivational' and 'inspirational' fables – will be accessed by the unconscious simply by reading them and letting the words and the ideas flow across, within and through you.

This is especially true of the poems.

You will also find ideas, concepts and/or phrases that will set you thinking about yourself, of your history and of how you function, individually and in relationship with others.

Take time to reflect on these, talk to those close to you, write about them; they could also be the seeds to change and growth.

Introductions, discussions, personal and clinical stories

For each of the pieces I have included introductions, discussions, personal and clinical stories.

The personal and clinical stories are included to help you to see that certain behaviours and problems are experienced by many people, myself included, and that they can all be resolved to some point or other.

My own stories are autobiographical and reflect my own life events; they are solely included to show that someone fairly normal and healthy can experience situations related to each and every one of the chapters.

On re-reading these stories, I have realised that one can easily find oneself with the impression that I am some kind of ascended master/hero/genius; this is of course far from the truth.
Although the situations and events are real, they are very carefully chosen to re-enforce the positive messages in each chapter. I have had at least as many errors and failures as I have had successes.

The clinical vignettes are compilations of or specific therapies with many personal details slightly changed to protect the patients' identities, but all are based on real cases that I have followed.

The improvements in the patients' situations are based on a certain therapeutic work – one session of hypnosis might prove to be a pivotal moment within the psychotherapeutic process, however much preparatory work would still need to have been done before.

The introductions and discussions are to explain the thinking behind the piece, to give some theoretical notions that might be of interest and use and to suggest ideas and pointers for your own personal use.

By reading this book you think to access somehow, parts of yourself that you have not been able to access before, in a way that things can change.

This is possible, and through using this book you might well access these other parts of yourself, and things can change.

However, this is not a book of magic; there are no supernatural powers associated with the words or formulas written within. Nor is it meant to replace a therapeutic process; there are no answers or space for the elaboration of deep questions or past events.

What this book contains are (just) some stories and poems. On reading and imagining the contents of these, parts of yourself will be able to contact with the message(s) contained within.

If there is a way – without much effort, simply, naturally – for there to be a change within those parts of yourself, to move, to grow, to unblock, to free, to advance, then that can start to take place. And the other changes in your external reality will follow, as is appropriate for you.

IMPORTANT NOTE:

This book is **not** intended as a sort of 'do-it-yourself-psychic surgery', if at any moment you start to feel unwell, stop what you are reading immediately and go and find something else to occupy yourself with and, if necessary, go and seek someone to be with.

Part 1: The Stories and Poems

1: The Safe Place

1.1
Elsa is nineteen years, a little awkward, a little overweight; not the most attractive of young ladies. She comes from a working-class background; her father is a factory worker. Elsa has been traumatised; she tends to feel very inhibited around boys unless she has had quite a lot to drink. Some weeks ago she got very drunk and when walking home with a friend they both had a sexual encounter with some boys. Elsa doesn't remember anything and her friend thinks that maybe she was forced. She has problems sleeping and feels very uncomfortable around men.

Could hypnosis help her remember?

The first step in most trauma work is to teach her to find her 'safe place' so that if at any of the experiences she remembers are too difficult, she can immediately 'switch' to something safe and secure.

2.1
Catherine is a middle-aged patient that I have been following for some time for anxiety problems. She has a difficult relationship with her mother who is dying in hospital with a lung insufficiency; she is being kept alive with bottled oxygen, either in an oxygen tent or with a mask. Being of a very strong character she wishes to choose the moment of her own death.

Catherine is in the process of making peace with her mother but is very worried about watching her die. We find an 'anchor' (a physical movement or contact) that will allow her to contact to her 'safe place'.

3.1

I am with my own therapist, he is about to work with me on my experiences of being abandoned as a young child by using hypnosis.

As is his habit, he first 'takes' me to my safe place. My safe place is the experience of flying, often through and above forests.

I am fascinated how my unconscious can create the physical and visual impressions that I am experiencing, I soar through the tree tops…

The Safe Place

The safe place is the 'classic' hypnotic induction for many therapists. It is often the first experience of hypnosis and EMDR work that they share with their clients and many will begin each and every session with it.

The safe place is a way to (re-) connect with an experience of well being (as mentioned briefly above.) This experience may be linked with an experience in the present or the past, in reality or in fantasy. It could be linked to situation or place, alone or with others.

However, it might, on the other hand, be just a positive feeling related to a single sensation; the feel of a certain material, the smell of a person or animal or place, a taste, a colour, the sensation of something warm or cool or wet or dry, or stillness or movement, a sound, a voice, a song, etc., etc.

This contact point may remain your only and specific entry point to these good feelings, or you might notice that they change in time or due to need or circumstances; it is for you to discover.

Whatever type of experience the 'safe place' is for you, what is important is that the experience brought on is a positive experience in which you feel good and safe.

This induction can be practiced almost anywhere and at any time of the day. Find yourself a 'quiet' corner, concentrate on your breathing, allow your eyes to close and let one or more of your senses lead you into your safe place…

The Safe Place

There is a place that doesn't exist
Or maybe it does
It might be real
And now
Or in the past
Or yet to be.

Where I feel safe
       Where I feel good
          Where I can let go
             Where I know I should

Where I am at home
       Where I can be free
          Where I can relax
             Where I can be me

A place I have been
Or heard of
Or seen
In a book
In a song
In a film
In a dream.

To be home
To be free
To relax
To be me

A place all alone
Or with friends
Or with kin
A part of outdoors
Or totally within

I'm safe
        I'm good
                I let go, like
                        I should

Or maybe a feeling
The sensation of flight
Or floating on water
The cool of the night

I'm home
        I'm free
                I relax
                        I am me

The smell of the ocean
A hot, red, spiced wine
Mother's perfume
A forest of pine

Safe
        Good
                Like
                        I should

A colour that calms you
A taste that fulfils
A texture caresses
A song deeply thrills

Home
     Free
         Relax
            Me

Safe, at home

     Feeling goo

I can relax

   Like I should

     Just

        Being

          Me.

1.2
Elsa had been sexually abused by the young man but she was also partly responsible as she had initiated the meeting and had led him on to a certain degree.

Remembering what had happened, although not comfortable, has helped her feel safer around men and has relieved her sleep problems.

The session had taken the full hour and we had benefited from the 'safe place', to which we returned several times during the process.

2.2
Catherine's mother held her hand and looked into her eyes before removing her oxygen mask. With her dying breaths she said the words that Catherine had waited her whole life to hear: 'I love you.'

Catherine linked her own hands together, which was her hypnotic anchor and lovingly and peacefully watched as her mother faded from this life.

3.2
My session ends. It was quite difficult and stressful.

Although I didn't return to my safe place during that session, however, just knowing that it is there, and that I can access it, is often enough to get me through.

Discussion:

The 'safe place' is an exercise that can be practiced in any type of situation where one wishes to connect with a feeling of well-being.

As stated above, it is not limited to any one type of experience, nor is one limited to that one experience.

You might find different things that bring you specific positive feelings which benefit you in certain situations and that which you most need at that time.

It is an experience to bring you peace and pleasure, something that we all need from time to time. Perhaps now would be a good time to enjoy that.

2: The Shoemaker and the Elves

1.1

Lucia has panic attacks. They seem to come from nowhere or in the most unlikely moments, such as at Christmas or on birthdays.

Lucia is 53, small and wiry, her tight, black curly hair is heavily streaked with grey; if anything, she looks older than her years.

She explains she and her husband came to Switzerland from Italy when they were a young couple, with the clear project of earning enough money to build themselves a nice home in their native village.

They both worked herculean hours, often doing two jobs in tandem, for the next 25 years.

Even having three children hardly slowed down their work rhythm. The children were often looked after by neighbours or other family members who were also in Switzerland, but quite soon it fell to the oldest daughter as soon as it was considered that she responsible enough – from when she was about 10 years old.

Although they would often meet up and eat *en famille* on weekends and festive occasions and would return 'home' to Italy for quite long holidays, the children complained sorely about the general absence of their parents.

Some years ago, Lucia and her husband left Switzerland to live in their beautiful home in Italy as planned, but after only two years they both realised that they could not cope with living in Italy.

However, since returning, Lucia has found the relationship between herself and her children very difficult. She feels that she has somehow wrecked the only real thing of value in her life – her family.

2.1

He is totally punctual. My buzzer rings at exactly 10:00 a.m. His expensive suit, easy manner and firm handshake announce someone confident and successful.

We exchange pleasantries, he sits with a relaxed, flowing motion, crosses his legs, joins the tips of his fingers together and gently smiles.

The assistant director of a local multinational company has learned how to put others at their ease, however, his eyes are not relaxed; the pupils are quite small, the eyes dart in one direction and then another. David is 56 years old, tall, a little on the thin side, hair thinning and greying, divorced and once again in the middle of a romantic rupture, he is not comfortable in this situation.

Being good looking, of a good local family and socially and professionally appreciated, he has always been able to attract women. He was married for a while, but even having children had not kept him faithful and sooner or later each woman had bored of his infidelities and had left.

'I'm getting old and I've wasted one opportunity after another to have a decent life as part of a couple. I'm clearly not capable of committing to that. I'll finish old and alone.'

I assure him then and there that he has the means, within himself, to change that.

3.1

I was living in a small, old caravan, in the North of Scotland, in the middle of winter. Yes, I was to some degree living and working (part time), in the community of Findhorn, but I was in reality unemployed and my professional career had totally stalled.

By that time, I had both an honours degree in Management Sciences and a City & Guilds certificate in Computer Programming. However, I had never worked using my degree qualifications and my limited computing skills, such as they were, were becoming very quickly completely out-of-date.

I had totally wasted the resources that I had taken so much time and effort to acquire.

The Shoemaker and the Elves

This is classic story that most of us have heard at some time or other in our lives. It's the story of how an old, poor shoemaker, wishing to make shoes or, in some versions, good-luck elves as Christmas presents for the poor orphans of the village is helped by the elves with his tasks.

But how did he become poor? Why was he so late with his tasks? How and why did he attract the elves to help at that time? And most importantly – what has all that got to do with you?!

It is supposed to be true that there exist individuals who 'do not have a selfish bone in their entire body' – not that I have ever met one. We are all a little selfish from time to time; it's quite human, and it's even necessary and healthy to protect one's health and happiness.

Sometimes, and in some situations, we feel that we should have more, that we don't have enough for ourselves. We then begin to organise our lives and those of others to compensate against this feeling of 'not enough', clearly more for our own comfort than for the common good. This in turn leads us into the downward spiral of meanness and lack.

When we are caught in the grip of a negative whirlpool, where it appears that we are constantly giving more than we receive. The way out seems to be to protect ourselves more and more.

Unfortunately, this strategy rarely works and the problem often worsens – a situation frequently seen in situations of couple conflict.

In this case, the real solution, very much in line with many religious and spiritual teachings, is to break the negative spiral by...*giving*.

Giving openly, giving freely, giving without any thought of appreciation, recognition or recompense.

Yes, it doesn't seem to make that much sense, but strangely enough, often it's the only thing that works.

Think on this

    And

        Enjoy the story.

The Shoemaker and the Elves
After the story by the brothers Grimm

Once upon a time, somewhere not so far away, nor so long ago, there was a shoemaker. The shoemaker came from a good family, and as a child he wanted for little. His parents wished for him to study, or join the army or the church, but the young man was drawn to the trade of shoemaker. He loved the feel and smell of the beautiful soft, fine leathers with which he worked and delighted in the challenge of creating just the right curve to accentuate the effect of an intricate stitch, which in turn would be of exactly the right size and strength to hold the material perfectly together and yet stay delicate and light.

The shoemaker found his perfect match in a refined young woman of the village, likewise of an artistic yet practical nature, as she had taken on the training of a seamstress.

And so they married, set up a home, and their respective businesses together.

And life was good. They had plenty of money, both being from good families, they enjoyed and were good at their respective trades, and they were appreciated by their clients.

And they enjoyed their good life. They lived well, eating and drinking only the very best of everything, taking long holidays and generally having a really good time. They also decided not to have children, as that would have greatly restricted their freedom to give pleasure to each other and themselves. They were not particularly selfish or mean, they just didn't choose to make the effort to go out of their way to help others.

After quite some years of this merry life, the couple noticed several things; that they were less and less motivated to work at their crafts; that their clients were less and less satisfied with the service given by the couple (many holidays and a 'so-what?'-attitude meant that the shop was often closed and orders always late) and, worst of all, there was less and less money to spend, as they had both spent heavily out of the capital of their inheritances.

So the shoemaker decided to take on an apprentice; his wife had long since ceased to practice her own profession. An apprentice would make sure that the shop was open regularly, make the shoes on time and bring in extra money.

And so the shoemaker took on an apprentice. He was a tall, willowy lad named Jake, dark and very serious looking, but with a certain artistic way of moving and a sweet, nervous smile. 'Why do you want to be my apprentice?' the shoemaker had asked him, during his interview. 'Why, to make shoes, of course, to create with the leather beautiful objects.' And his eyes widened with pleasure of the thought of the work.

The shoemaker invested himself with the task of teaching his enthusiastic protégé all that he knew of his craft, while his wife kept shop and once again things went well.

After just one year, Jake was more than capable of making any kind of shoes that one could wish for or imagine. The shoemaker and his wife were well satisfied, and planned themselves a long holiday, a very long holiday; after all, they had worked particularly hard for quite some time and had done well with the business.

They took themselves off for a wonderful six-month holiday, happy in the thought that while they were enjoying themselves, the business was looking after itself. Thus it only hurt and surprised them more, when after only two months, they received an urgent message from their bank informing them that if they didn't put some money in their account straight away, no bills would be paid that month.

They hurried home immediately only to find that the door of the shop was locked, and had to be opened with the shoemaker's own spare key. 'What could have happened?' they asked themselves. They went straight into the workshop at the back, and what do you think they saw there? Why, Jake, of course, lost in the creation of an exquisite pair of black pigskin court shoes. 'What is happening?' demanded the shoemaker. 'I'm making shoes,' replied Jake, lost in admiration of his own creation. 'But why is the shop door locked?' inquired the Shoemakers' wife. 'People kept coming in and disturbing me in my work, so eventually I had to lock the door to keep them out.' Jake just couldn't understand that the work included dealing with people. In fact he was very, very scared of talking to people that he didn't know. And so, quite reluctantly, the Shoemaker had to let him go.

The shoemaker and his wife thought hard before taking on another apprentice. They eventually took on a bright looking lad named David, who had black, slicked-back hair and an easy, cheerful manner. 'Do you like people and selling?' the wife had insisted on asking during the first meeting with the young man. 'Nothing better, nothing better,' he said and smiled back at her with a cheeky grin.

The Shoemaker's wife was well taken with the young man, and so they took him on.

Once again the couple invested heavily in the training of the apprentice, but this time the Shoemakers' wife insisted that David spent a lot a time in the shop, meeting the customers, talking to them and selling the shoes. In fact he was excellent at it; 'Such a charming young fellow;' 'So very polite;' 'always so available.' In fact, he was so good in the shop that it seemed a waste to force him to spend too much time in the workshop – although, of course, the Shoemaker also put a great deal of effort into teaching him the craft.

And so, after another year of intense effort, it seemed that David was ready to be left to his own devices, and the Shoemaker and his wife prepared themselves for a well-deserved vacation.

This time the Shoemaker really did need to take some time off, as he had totally exhausted himself by making his shoes and teaching David at the same time, who, though a really nice chap, was not at all gifted in the trade of cobbler.

And so they left, only to be called back once again by an urgent note from their banker.

Again they arrived home to find the shop closed up, only this time there was no apprentice, only a vast pile of shoes heaped up behind the counter. 'What's this?' exclaimed the Shoemaker, and, on examining the shoes, 'What's *this*?' he cried. For the shoes were of the very worst quality. It didn't take much thinking to work out what had happened; David was more than good enough at selling shoes, but when it came to making them, he was a disaster!

But things were much, much worse than that. He had spent the money that the people had paid for the shoes to redecorate the shop, and when the customers had demanded their money back he had to go to the bank to take out most of the rest of the money in the Shoemaker's account to pay them back their money.

He had also used up almost all the leather in the stock, and as he had no money, he hadn't paid the tanners and they didn't want to give any credit. After all, the whole town knew of the very bad quality of the Shoemaker's shoes now, and nobody would dream of going to him for shoes anymore. David, of course, had run away in shame, and that suited everybody very well.

The shoemaker and his wife were ruined!

He had no more energy; they had wasted all their resources.

And now, just to add to the wretchedness of it all, soon it would be Christmas.

The shoemaker felt old and sick and tired. 'We're at the bottom of the bottom, there is nothing left in me,' he complained bitterly. Just then, by chance, he looked out of his window, and saw a little girl in rags looking in at him.

'What do you want?' he asked roughly, opening the door.

'Just to wish you "merry Christmas,"' replied the girl, bursting into tears, and running off, her little bare feet, leaving uneven prints in the snow.

The Shoemaker looked back at his wife, both feeling hurt and shocked by what had happened. 'Come on,' she said, putting on her shawl, 'let's see if we can find her.' They hurried out of the shop, into the falling snow. The little footprints were quickly being hidden away under the increasing blanket of fresh snow. As they turned a narrow corner, the wind picked up, hurling freezing darts of misery into their faces.

'I can't go on,' she whimpered, but yet they did. Old and pitiful they looked, fighting through the increasingly resisting snow. Step by step they battled on, as if their own lives depended on finding the inner force to catch up to the little urchin girl.

Finally, they arrived at the door of a little, old, dishevelled building, in the poorest part of town. It was the village orphanage. They shook the snow off their shoes, pushed open the worn, splintered door and entered into the gloomy half-darkness.

The place might have been grey, cold and damp, but just the same, it was full of life and activity. Ten, fifteen, twenty children – it was impossible to keep track of how many there were – were in the process of decorating the hall for Christmas.

It seemed that the children had begged whatever they could from the kind-hearted citizens of the village; bits of cloth and ribbon, old clothes, toys, candles, all sorts of bric-a-brac, and with these treasures they were preparing for Christmas.

Suddenly, one of the children noticed the Shoemaker and his wife, and as if an ice-cold wave washed over them, the children stopped, lined up and waited. Heads down, they stood in silence.

They didn't know what they had done wrong this time, but they were ready to accept their punishment. These resilient little beings, like young saplings expecting to be whipped by the storm, to be pushed, bent and pressured; yet, thanks to some secret, deep, inner force, able to resist, to spring back, to still be in a state of wonder and excitement for this feast of new beginnings.

The old couple looked down the line of bowed heads and bare feet. The shoemaker, after so many years of plying his trade, couldn't stop himself from noticing each pair of feet, the sizes and the shapes, it was now a type of reflex for him. His wife, who was much more used to looking at peoples' faces, pointed out the little girl, hidden between two bigger boys.

As the Shoemaker walked slowly towards her, she shrank a little back behind the boys, although not leaving the line. One could almost see her little heart beating furiously through the flimsy cotton of her shabby dress, and the wispy body underneath.

The Shoemaker bent down, just a little. 'I just wanted to say that I'm sorry that I shouted at you and scared you.' He took a small coin out of his pocket and folded it into her small, shaking hand.

She was much too upset to respond, but as the two adults turned to leave, one of the bigger boys, the one on the left, called out, 'Thank you!' and then, like a chorus of nightingales all the children sang out, 'Thank you, merry Christmas.'

The couple struggled their difficult way home, the wicked snow slapping their exposed skin, and stinging their eyes. When they eventually closed the door behind them, it looked as if they had both been crying.

They didn't speak. She went up to kitchen and put on some water to make tea. He went into his workshop and hunted out every piece of leather that he could find. 'Is there enough?' she asked softly, bringing in his cup. 'Yes, yes, I think so, maybe just enough.'

And so he took down his old oil lamp, tapered the wick and together they began the impossible task of making sixteen pairs of shoes before morning.

First, he drew out each pattern, remembering exactly the shape and size of each foot. She then cut out the leather, being extra, extra careful, as there was no spare leather to make another. Then, he would put them on the last, stretch and stitch. Slowly their eyes began to close, and yet they seemed to carry on, there and not there at the same time; asleep, yet totally functional. Time and space warped and bent. Were they stitching while in their dreams or were they dreaming that they were stitching?

The crowing of the red, farm cock awoke them with a start. '*Did* we?' they both asked together, looking round.

Two by two they counted the pairs of shoes – fourteen, fifteen, sixteen! Quickly they piled the shoes into an old sack and he rushed out of the shop.

Not looking where he was going, the Shoemaker bumped heavily into an elegant woman rushing the other way, knocking both of them down.

'I'm so dreadfully sorry.' apologised the Shoemaker, but the woman didn't respond. She was too busy examining the pairs of shoes that had fallen out the sack.
'What exquisite little shoes,' she exclaimed, 'who made them?'
'I did, of course,' the old man retorted

The woman took a moment to reply. She was reflecting on something. 'Could you possibly make me a pair of shoes by tomorrow morning, I would pay you very well for your trouble?'

Now it was the turn of the Shoemaker to be silent.
The woman continued, as if in explanation, 'I received a puppy this morning for Christmas and first thing that did was to chew up the shoes that I was going to wear tomorrow at the Duke's ball. I was rushing to see if I could find a cobbler that would be open today to make them, as I have to leave first thing in the morning to get there.'

'But what about the choice of leather?'
'That is not a problem. My husband knows a tanner, and he is taking my old shoes, so as to get a perfect match.'
'I have to deliver these shoes, but yes, yes, I'll do it!'

Of course, making a pair a slippers for the Duke's Ball was a little more complicated than making simple shoes for the orphans, and the Shoemaker was already very tired from his work the previous night, but as they didn't even have enough money for food, he really had no choice.

It was late in the afternoon when the tanner eventually delivered the leather.

And so, once again, he took down his old lantern and prepared himself to work through the night. He did his very, very best to stay awake, and even dreamt that he was still working, but even so, when the cock crowed he knew that he had failed and had fallen asleep. He was still in the process of waking himself up when he heard some-one knocking at his door.

'Oh, cobbler, cobbler, are you there?'

'Woe is me', he muttered to himself, preparing to have to go and apologise to the lady for not succeeding in finishing the shoes on time. Just then, out of the corner of his eye, he noticed that they seemed quite finished. There he was, lost in thought, when the lady rushed in, closely followed by the Shoemaker's wife, who had finally opened the door.

'Why they are gorgeous! You are so clever, and so quick! I didn't really believe that it was possible. I'm going to tell everybody what a wonderful find I've made in you.' And so off she went, after generously paying him for his work and then organising for some more leather to be delivered that very day for another three new pairs of shoes to be made for her for the following week.

Over breakfast, the Shoemaker told his wife his experience of the previous night.

'It's as if there was someone or something else that came to help me when I really needed it,' he admitted to her, feeling like maybe he was just a little crazy.

'And how are you going to find out who or what that just might be?'
'I'll...I'll stay up tonight, and hide, and watch.'

'You are a crazy old man! You haven't slept properly in days – how do you think you'll manage that?'

'I'll do it anyway.'

And so that night, the Shoemaker hid himself away behind a counter, and waited to see what he might see. And he waited and he waited and he waited. And eventually he fell asleep.

'Wake up, wake up! I told you that you wouldn't make it, silly old man!'

'No, no I *did* see them.'

'In a dream?'

'I…I'm not sure; maybe it was a dream, maybe not.'

'So, tell me, what did you see?'

'I saw two little creatures – yes that was it! – two little creatures, a man and a woman. They were very, very small, like, you know, like little elves.'

'Oh yes, and what did these two elves look like?'

'Well, like us, yes, just like us, like you and me.'

'Well, of course!' screamed his wife, holding her sides and laughing. 'Who else in this world or the next is there to help us, if not ourselves?'

And so, as you might imagine, the Shoemaker restarted his business, which became quite successful again, but as he and his wife were getting quite old, they took on some help; someone to help him make the shoes, someone for the shop to help sell them and someone to help around the house.

The Shoemaker, his wife, Jake, David and the little orphan girl (who they later adopted), all lived very happily ever after.

1.2

Lucia has seen and accepted the point of view of her children that they have felt, and not totally unreasonably, to have been abandoned by their parents all their lives.

The parents have apologised to their three children and have asked if it could be possible to 'make amends.'

Two of the three children have accepted to have two very motivated and available babysitters for their own children.

2.2

We are in a couple setting. David is wearing an old jumper with a hole in elbow; Doris is gently making fun of him. David had asked to try to use her potter's wheel and had succeeded to cover himself in wet clay.

It had been a pretty tough 18 months for David and I, but as David had stated early on in the therapy, 'When I really set my mind to accomplishing something, sooner or later I will accomplish it.' And now here we are.

3.2

'What would you like to do with your life?'
The question was simple yet profound.
'I've always liked helping over people. Oh yes, and I like to talk.'
'So why not become a psychologist?'
At the age of 38 I enrolled in the University of Lausanne to study psychology.
I am now a successful psychologist, helping people put their lives back in order, enjoying a challenging and fulfilling professional life.

Discussion:

This fable is concerned with our abilities to contact our own inner resources. We all start out in life with a vast store of inner riches, as both did the shoemaker and his wife. Unfortunately, through bad luck (sickness, inappropriate parenting, external events) or some foolishness (those woes that we bring on ourselves), we often end up without access to them.

Often we feel that we have no more strength to do what we need to carry on or to rebuild ourselves or our lives, or even worse, that we have no more right to this energy or happiness.

These feelings are our true feelings, but the reality is otherwise; there are always those other parts of ourselves that are strong and available; we just have to allow ourselves to believe in them and to call on them.

The orphan children were still in contact with them, even in their terrible life situations. The shoemaker and his wife forced their passage through the snow, calling on that strength, and the magical elves were only the same forces again.

We all get down sometimes. Life can be really, really tough, but when we dig deep enough into our own miraculous pockets there is always a little more to be found.

3: Arranging the Attic

1.1
Margaret is passed middle age, slightly overweight, speaks quite slowly and is heading towards a depression.

She is about to fall victim to the 'empty nest' syndrome.

Her main occupation for the last 25 years has been that of 'home-maker', looking after her husband and five children.

Sam, her husband, works long hours and is involved with local politics and Sylvie, her youngest child, is now about to leave home.

Margaret is facing an empty future.

2.1
Carl is confused. Now, all of us can feel confused at times, but Carl is 'always' confused.

He is a good-looking young man of 19; very polite, neatly dressed, short tidy hair. In short, a 'good boy.'

He is about to start his third attempt at an apprenticeship. At the beginning of each of his first two apprenticeships he had been convinced that he had found his chosen calling, but after only a few months he had realised that the profession was not for him.

3.1

When living near Liverpool I was employed by a company to do some data entry on a short-term project in Humberside.

When I arrived to start the project I was informed by the manager that the project had been delayed and that I was just to hang around their office until they needed me.

I noticed that they had a room in which there was a single computer that people would use from time to time. I asked what the computer was used for and was told that they had paid an independent programmer to write a custom programme for them but it had never worked properly and the original programmer couldn't seem to sort out the problems.

I asked in which language the program had been written and as the response was 'Basic.' As I had a little experience in using that language, I asked if they minded if I would try to see if I could access the programme.

I did succeed in accessing the programme, but it was in a version that I didn't know and there were hundreds of pages of code.

To say that I was lost and out of my depth didn't even come close…

Arranging the Attic

Many of us feel at one time or other that we are of little value, that we don't fit in, that we are stupid, ugly, uninteresting, useless and/or that there is nothing about ourselves, or that we can say or do, that is of any value.

There are also times when we feel confused, unable to think clearly, unable to organise or structure certain jobs or situations or in extreme circumstances - our lives.

How or why this has come about is not important.

Maybe you have lost something or someone important in your life; a relationship that has finished poorly, an important project that you invested in or a job that has not worked out.

Maybe you have carried a feeling or impression of not being good enough for as long as you can remember.

Maybe you are being forced with choices or decisions that seem impossible to make.

Maybe everything seems too complicated and complex (this can perhaps be either a cause of or the effect of a depression), and you cannot see even how to start to sort out what you have to do.

Of course there are no magic solutions. However, there are one or two reflections which might be worth reflecting upon:

We all have facets of ourselves which are of value; who we are, how we are, what we can do.

Allow yourself to relax into a neutral state, listen to some calming music, take a quiet walk and/or just read the story. Than write down anything and everything that you can think of that is positive about yourself (you can, of course, ask for help if you have people about you who could do so.)

From this list, which can be long or short – often the first time you try, the list is *very* short but don't stop there – repeat the exercise a few times.

From this list you will notice that you are someone with resources, someone of value, someone that can organise and overcome your difficulties and problems and can be appreciated by yourself and by others.

Remember; most problems, even if they seem so complicated that there is no solution, need often only to be looked at from a different angle to be solvable. That angle is usually linked to giving up something that seems too important or even impossible to give up or doing something that seems equally impossible for you to do.

Remember;

> Difficult jobs can take a long time,

> ***Impossible jobs can take just a little longer***

And only way to walk a thousand miles is to take the first step and the second and …

Arranging the Attic

Maurice was not what one would call a handsome young man. For a start, his ears were too big, and his face was too long, a sort of rounded oblong shape. The boys in school mocked him often, they called him 'Kettle' – some vague reference to a kettle drum, it seems. They even pulled his ears, which made them sore, but you could not tell, as they would already be bright red from his blushing with embarrassment.

He took to running away from their mocking voices. They would chase after him for a while, but Maurice would run into the woods where it was difficult under foot, and so they would soon become bored of trying to capture him and stop, but his anger and his tears would keep him running and running and running. Finally he would quieten down only to often find himself miles and miles from home, and it could take him hours to return there. It was fortunate that his parents often worked quite late, so that they didn't know at what time he sometimes arrived at their small, ordered semi-detached house.

Maurice was not a boy whose parents didn't care for him; his parents loved him and supported him in their own ways, but they did not succeed in helping him face his problems with the other children. They would offer platitudes like: 'children can be mean like that' or 'we are as we are, and we need to learn to live with what we have,' etc.) He was never neither particularly bright nor particularly confident, but over time, because of the continual little torments from the other young scholars, he started to become more and more reserved, and his school results started gently to descend.

As his parents were neither very social, nor had they had the opportunity to go very far in their respective schooling, they didn't notice much was wrong.

And so time passed, until one day Maurice was walking home from school when an old woman turned and screamed at him, 'Come here boy!'

Now he was quite used to being told off by people that he knew, but this old woman he had never had anything to do with - and for good reason. The old woman in question was known as a sort of a witch, not at all a real witch, but someone weird and unpleasant. Maurice wanted to run away, but something within him, some inner force, turned him around, and directed his feet towards the old hag.

'I have something for you that you want and need.'

'I don't know what you're talking about. What do I want and need?'

'Don't you know?'

'A magic potion to make me big and strong and to make my ears smaller.' He didn't know what possessed him to speak like this to her; aggressively, yet very honest.

'Strange as it may seem to you, young man, but contrary to what certain spiteful women might say, I am not a practising witch, so stirring magic potions is not on the menu.'

'Okay, then I don't know what I want and need that you can give me.'

'I want you to tidy up my attic for me.'

'What?'

'You heard what I said. Saturday morning, nine o'clock; don't be late.'

'But why should I do that for you?'

'I've already told you.'

'But I don't know what it is that I want and need.'

'Somewhere you do, somewhere you do. Don't be late – I can't abide lateness.' And so she left.

Maurice knew where the old woman lived, of course, everyone did. She was well known to all the community. Her house was a hovel; old, run down, the garden madly overgrown through years and years of inattention, and he arrived there just as the village clock started to chime the hour.

The front door was already open when he got there. Maurice debated with himself whether to go inside or not. He was scared that entering without being invited to would be considered as very rude and that he would be told off. On the other hand, the door being left open was a clear invitation for him to enter and therefore not doing so would also be a form of rudeness.

'Well, it's nine o'clock, are you coming in or not?'

'Yes, yes, I'm coming in.' The small house was surprisingly cosy once inside, although it must be admitted that Maurice did feel a little claustrophobic, due to the fact that all the walls were totally filled with old pictures and embroideries. The embroideries were of all subjects; flowers, animals – mainly dogs – even people. A Spanish dancer caught his attention. She had red lips, black hair, a red rose in her mouth, and a black and red dress pulled up over her knee, showing a full white set of petticoats and a long, long dancer's leg.

'Next time you leave, take your body with you!'
'What?'

'You were day-dreaming.'

  'I think that I do it a lot. I'm often told off at school for day-dreaming.'
'Then you must be doing it badly.'
'Badly?'
'Day-dreaming is an art; it should be done well, or not at all.'

Maurice looked closely at the old woman. Was she mocking him or was she being serious?

Again Maurice found himself voicing his thoughts without the customary control that we usually exercise.

'Are you being serious?'

'Young man, I am always serious. Would you like a cup of tea before starting work?'

Maurice, being a little scared of this strange woman, preferred to be out of her presence as quickly as possible.

'No thank you, I've just finished my breakfast.'

'Good, we can then start.'

Maurice, silently breathed a sigh of relief and turned back towards the door that led out to the hall where stood the staircase.

'And just where do you think that you are off to now?'

'To the attic, to tidy the attic.'

'And what payment have we agreed that you will receive for this service?'

'What I want and need?' He hadn't forgotten that part of their conversation from the week - even though he hadn't the slightest idea what that might mean.

'And just what do you want and need?'

'I don't have the slightest idea.'

'Then what good is going upstairs now?'

Maurice felt like the room was getting smaller and small, all the faces of the animals and people seemed to be closing in on him, even the Spanish dancer seemed to wink at him. She did seem serious.

'Sit down.' He did. 'Now, what do you want and need?'

'I don't know.'

'Maybe you should try to think once in a while.'

'I am thinking.'

'Well then, stop thinking. Just let those parts of you that know react.'

'What?'

'So, what do you need?' Maurice shook his head.

'All right, what do you want?'

To leave, to run away, he thought, but said, 'I don't know.' He was even starting to feel a little angry. What did she want with him, this crazy woman? He should never have agreed to come here in the first place. She was clearly mad, but was she also dangerous? Should he try to make a run for it?

'What would you like?'

'I don't know.' She was standing between him and the door, but she looked quite frail, like he could just push her out of the way.

'Well then, what don't you like?'

'People making fun of me.' There, it was out.

'Who makes fun of you?' He bit his tongue.

'People.'

'Which people?' Well, he could say it now.

'The boys – the boys make fun of me.'

'So, what would you like?'

'For the boys to stop making fun of me.' Somehow it felt good to say it, even to this crazy old woman. 'I would very much like for the boys to stop making fun of me.'

'And what would you need so that they stopped making fun of you?'

'Something to make them like me.'

'And what sort of thing would make them like you?'

'If I could do something special.'

'Okay, are there any other people whose attitudes you'd like to change?'

'Well, there are the teachers, they think that I'm stupid.'

'Are you stupid, Maurice?' He started to go bright red.

'No, no, I'm not stupid, it's, it's just I sort of get lost. It's okay at home; there's no one there, and I can do things, but when I'm at school, I sort of just drift off, like I don't want to be there. Yeah, I know, no one really likes school, well just the swots and creeps, but, but somehow it's different, it's like I need to get away. And then the teachers, they notice, and they ask me questions that they know I can't answer, and then I start to feel bad, and I get hot, and then, and then...' Maurice stopped speaking, the emotions were too strong, and painful. All the moments of awful embarrassment came to him; going red, everybody looking at him, most of the boys clearly enjoying his discomfort, mocking, 'Go on, Kettle, see how red you can get!'

'So?'

'So, I'd like to be able to be more, more, I don't know, more present at school.'

'And how could you be more present at school, Maurice?'

'Maybe if I was good at something. Yeah, if there was something that I was really, really good at in school, then I'd maybe feel better, and the boys wouldn't laugh, and the teachers might be nicer, and then I'd feel good, and then it'd be okay.'

'So, Maurice, your demands are to be able to do something special, so that the other boys respect you, and to succeed at school?'

'Yeah, I suppose so, but...'

'No buts, Maurice.'

'But, but it's impossible.'

'My poor, poor boy, you really don't know how to dream. What time is it?' She looked at the big clock on the wall, its pendulum swinging gently to and fro. 'We've still the whole day ahead of us. Maurice, you see the pendulum on the clock, swinging one way and then the other?'

He dumbly nodded his head. 'Watch.' She walked up to it, put her hand out and stopped it in full swing. 'Our attention is like this pendulum; at one moment it can be here,' she swung it full to the right. 'This is when we are fully awake, concentrating, totally present. Now, here,' and she swung it to the other extreme,

'Here is where we are fully unconscious, asleep. Now most of the time, we are somewhere near the middle; conscious of our surroundings, yet also in contact with our deeper thoughts. I say something, here, now, in the present, here and now, and for a moment or two that makes you think of something not here. When you spoke of your experiences at school, you were back there, re-experiencing, as if here and now you are also there then. But of course, you don't have to invoke negative images and experiences, you could also create positive ones.'

Maurice was having a bit of hard time following what she was talking about, and somehow in the manner of her speaking, he was finding himself starting to float off a little.
'Now, to really, really daydream properly,' she continued, 'What you need to be able to do is to be totally connected to the present and at exactly the same time to be in your other experience.
That way you can better control what and where you want to be.'

To be here and not here at the same time?' He was feeling confused, and yet it somehow didn't really matter. He was feeling strangely good at this moment, as if he were about to receive a wonderful present, there, wrapped, on his lap, opening all by itself. He was caught, fascinated, lulled by the old woman's gentle rocking voice.

'Yes, yes Maurice, that is exactly it! See, see how quick you are. You are really a very intelligent little boy. And you have a wonderful imagination, but, but I wonder... no, no maybe not...'

'Not what?'

'It's really quite difficult. Most people, even adults, can't do it.'

'Do what?'

'You see as the pendulum swings, forwards and backwards...' She released the object.

'Yes.'

'Some people are capable of imagining two pendulums; one going in one direction, and one going in the other direction, crossing here, at the bottom, and both reaching the top at the same moment.'

'Like this?' Maurice starting to swing his arms across his chest, crossing at his navel.

'Yes, yes, just like that.'

'You want me to look at the clock?'

'You can if you want to.'

'Can I swing my arms?'

'For as long as your arms wish to swing.'

The woman turned back towards the clock, gently smiling to herself. The pendulum was swinging gently, rhythmically there and back, there and back.

She reached out her hand, blocking its trajectory.

Once stopped, she re-centred her attention on the young boy seated in her front room, gently swinging his arms to and fro, to and fro, his eyes fixed in front, eyelids starting to droop.

'If your eyes wish to close, why not just let them? Maybe you will be able to see the pendulum even more easily.' His eyes closed, and almost immediately after, his arms ceased their movements.

'How are you feeling, Maurice?' There was no immediate response.

'…A bit sleepy.'

'But you know exactly where you are, don't you?'

Sure, I'm in your creepy house.' Maurice well knew that he shouldn't have said that, but he wanted to prove to himself that he was still in control of himself, even if he had accepted to do this weird thing, and that he could always stop whatever was happening if he should want to. Although, it did feel rather good, this sort of letting-go feeling….

'Now Maurice, we are here to learn how to daydream properly, okay?'

From the outside, one could get the impression that Maurice and the old women were like a television presenter talking to someone via satellite.

A question would be asked, the information would be sent by satellite, received a few seconds later by Maurice, he would respond, but we wouldn't hear the response until another few seconds had passed.

'Okay.'

'First daydream that the boys accept you.'

'Yes,' he responded a little quicker. 'But I don't see why or how.'

We'll leave that for your body and your unconscious to sort out later. What might be nice now, would be to experience the moment after you had done this good thing. Where would it be?'

'Coming out after school, I suppose. Yes, yes that would be it.'

'Can you see yourself coming out of school?'

'Yes, yes I can.'

'Tell me what is happening.'

'The boys are all there, and they're smiling, and they're chanting.'

'What are they chanting?' Maurice stopped a while, feeling a little embarrassed.

'…Ket-tle…Ket-tel…Ket-tel…'

The attic was an awful mess; there were crates and crates of things, piled any old how.

'But what do you want me to do with all this?'

'Arrange them.'

'But how, in what way?'

'Be creative.' And with that clear instruction, she left.

Maurice looked around. He was lost, confused, perplexed. His head mirrored the turmoil that massed before his eyes.

'What am I supposed to do with all this junk?' He suddenly felt exhausted, as if just the idea of the sheer enormity of the task had already tired him out. So he did what he always did when faced with a difficulty, he 'phased out.' He sat down in a space between two large, dusty crates, and let his mind wonder, half dreaming, half awake.

He thought of the scene in the film of the 'Sword in the Stone' when Arthur, then a miserable, little, mocked boy, watches Merlin, the magician, pack up his forest home by making all the objects come to life and pack themselves into Merlin's magic bag.

Magic bag, tidying up, yes…Mary Poppins, she had a magic carpet bag, and could tidy up using magic, and it was fun.

Sure, why not make some sort of game of it? He would challenge himself. How? A time challenge, he would have to do a certain bit of tidying up before lunch. Okay, what would be the first thing? He looked around himself, well, he couldn't think of sorting anything out because there was no room for anything.

Still half in his stupor, the image of Kermit talking to Miss Piggy came to mind. He really liked the Muppet Show. The arrogant lady pig was asking the hassled frog when he would do something. 'I don't have time,' he explained to her. 'Make time!' she would respond. Well I have no room to sort anything. 'Make room!' the lady pig in his head retorted. Okay, that's what I'll do. My challenge is to clear this half of the attic before lunch.

And so he set about moving the objects and boxes and heaving the heavy crates from the half where he would pile everything. First he took out all the small objects that where on the floor between the crates, then he pushed all the crates as tightly together as he could. Then he piled the small objects on top of the crates. He then took the smaller objects from the half that he was to clear, and piled these also, as much as possible onto the crates he had already moved. Finally he pushed the remaining crates towards the others and then piled the remaining smaller things on top.
'Phew,' he exclaimed out loud. 'Done it.'

The effort had really been considerable, but Maurice was so taken with his image of having succeeded his challenge, that nothing would stop him achieving what he had set himself out to do.
He looked around the attic, doubly satisfied; not only was one half of the space clear, but during this first moving of stuff, he had discovered some things that might be helpful for the next steps.

First of all he had found some cardboard boxes, flattened out, but when remade, they would be really good for sorting things into, either to keep or to throw out.

As well as those, he had found some boards with which had could make some shelves which would be great as book shelves, or some such thing.

'I'm going for lunch now.'
'Did you have a successful morning?'
'Yes, yes I did actually.'
'Good, will you be coming back this afternoon?' The question somewhere surprised him.
'Yes, of course I'm coming back this afternoon.'

On the way home, he realised that up until that very moment he hadn't thought about going for more than the one morning. Of course, it wasn't reasonable to think that he could tidy someone's attic in a few hours, even if it wasn't in the crazy state of that one, but the idea of going back a second time had never crossed his mind. Now, there was no question; he would return and keep returning until the job was done. And done it would be, done well.

Maurice started whistling to himself, he always did when he felt happy, only, when was the last time that he had felt like whistling?

Maurice knew that the rest of the tidying would take quite a long time, there was so much junk to sort out, but that didn't worry him. There was something about arranging that attic that was making him feel good, good about himself, and that was all that mattered.

Now that he had cleared one half of the attic, he first brushed it clean, then he made up some boxes to put things in, and then he built up some shelves for the books.

'Okay', he said to himself, 'now the real work starts.'
At first he had little idea how to proceed. The old woman either had no idea or chose to have no idea how he should organise things, so he started off a little lost.

After a while he sorted out a sort of a system. He had one box for things that were clearly junk, which would be thrown away without worry. Then he had a second box in which he placed all the things that might or might not be junk, which would have to be further sorted at a later date with the woman. The third box was for all the other things, the things that were clearly of value. Here he put all pictures, objects that looked valuable, little statuettes, tools and medals…
It was of course the medals that held the most interest. There were quite a lot a war medals from various past conflicts, but the ones that really caught his attention were for running. One could get a medal just for running? It somehow struck him as funny.

Why, he seemed to do nothing but run, morning, noon and night, and he could run fast; fast and for a long time.

And of course there were the books; cloth-bound, paperbacks, books in good condition and bad. There seemed to be books about just everything; lots and lots of novels, books on geography, history, biographies, autobiographies and, not that strangely seeing all the running medals, books about running.

After about an hour and a half, Maurice started to run out of steam. It was then that he gave himself permission to open some of the books.

The first few didn't hold his interest for more than a few moments, but the third, 'A History of Running,' drew him in.

There were chapters on ancient civilisations; prehistoric hunters, messengers, 'runners', the Olympics (of course), the four minute mile. There was information from Africa, Australia, North America, even Tibet.

What was awful, was that the book spoke of places and events that Maurice knew little or nothing about, but just the same, he was excited – very, very excited. He hunted around, yes, there was an old atlas – he dove into it, there, to the north of India, bordering on China, it was huge!

Suddenly, he noticed that it was getting dark, but how was that possible? There was no talk of a storm, and it was still early, it was only…seven o'clock! Seven o'clock, how on earth had it got to seven o'clock? He was in trouble, he was late for supper, and he had hardly done anything to the attic all day. He jumped up and ran down the stairs.

'Maurice.' He started.

'Yes?'

'Have you had a successful day?'

'I haven't finished yet.'

'I didn't ask you if you had finished, I asked if you had had a successful day.'

'Well, sort of, no, yes, yes, I think so.'

'Will I be seeing you again then?'

'I'm busy all week. Can I come back on Saturday?'

'Whenever you want to; the door will be on the latch; just let yourself in. Goodbye!

Saturday eventually arrived. Maurice was very keen to return to the attic.

He worked at tidying for the first few hours, then he stopped until lunch, reading the books and dreaming of being a great runner. Then he went home, ate and returned for the afternoon, two hours of work and more hours with the books.

The next day was much the same, only this time, Maurice brought with him a little note book in which to write, as there was so much interesting information that he wanted to remember, and there was much too much for him to memorise like that.

The tidying seemed to do itself; he became almost an independent observer of the re-organisation. Each day he would come almost as if just to see what new bit of the attic had been sorted during the day before. In several weeks the attic had been tidied three times! Each time more and more carefully, more and more deeply and more and more completely.

Little by little Maurice was becoming an expert on everything even remotely associated with running.

He had studied a little of the geography of each country mentioned; the physical terrain, mountains, valleys, deserts, rivers, as well as festivals, food and other basic living conditions that would affect a runner's life

. He also found that for many of the communist country's runners, their politics also had a great importance.

Politics was also important in other countries for different reasons, for blacks, aborigines and women. There was, of course, also the historical element to take into account. Each subject further fuelled his intellectual interest.

He found references to physiology, drugs, the psychology of sport, even clothing and commercial sponsorship found their place in his growing library of note books.

Maurice also found a desire to try a copy some of the great athletes that were pictured in various publications and, to his total astonishment, he found that he had a little talent for drawing the human figure.

For the outside observer, it will not be a great surprise that sooner or later this meteoric increase in academic knowledge would be remarked on at school. It was five or six weeks after Maurice had started to arrange the attic when the history teacher informed the class that they were about to study ancient Greece.
'Does anyone know anything about ancient Greece?' There was no response.
'Anything…?'
'Why don't you ask Kettle?'
'Maurice, do you know something about ancient Greece?'

He started as usual to feel bad, to feel flushed, to feel foolish, but then, but then – something clicked.
'Yes, yes, sir, I do.'
'Well?' There was an unexpected silence in the class. This was not the usual game. 'What do you have to share with the class?'
'That there was a lot of fighting between the Greeks and the Persians.'
'Yes, yes that's right. And would you have any idea of about what period that would cover?'
The general silence continued
'Well, well,' Maurice started to lose it for a moment, but no, he knew something and he could say it: 'About, about 500 BC.'

'Was there something special that you know of that happened at around that date?'

The other children of the class started looking at each other, there was something unusual happening here; a teacher was questioning Maurice, and he was answering!

'It was a battle, a big battle, the Greeks were fighting the Persians and they were outnumbered by a lot, and they won, and that's when the first marathon was run.'

'What, between the Greeks and Persians, during the war?'

'Thank you, Jones. You don't need to show off all your ignorance at once. In fact, Maurice is basically correct. The battle you speak of was the battle of Marathon, and a Greek soldier was sent to Athens to announce the victory. That historic run has since been re-established as the marathon for the Olympic games.'

The history class was only the first episode in the new story of Maurice's academic ascent. Geography was the next to experience the ever-widening knowledge base of the boy. From Tibet to Africa to South America, he had studied a little of all the countries that had produced runners of note.

When communism came up in political science, he had things to say; psychology appeared once in passing in a class of social sciences; the formula for time, distance and speed arrived in his maths class; human biology became a subject of strong interest for him, even in cookery class he managed to surprise his teacher with a clear understanding of nutrition and diet. He even impressed his art class with his new-found talent for drawing the human form. In short, his school image undertook a dramatic change, but this was nothing compared to reaction that he received when he found and joined the local cross-country running club.

It took him a little while to pluck up the courage to contact the club, and when he first arrived, some of the members didn't look very friendly, but when they saw him run, their attitudes soon improved.

He was fast and he could run and run and run.

****

'Kettle!'

'Yeah, what?'

'Me dad says that someone called Maurice, from our school won a race this weekend doing cross country running.'

'It was me!' The other boys soon realised that an inexhaustible runner could also be useful for other sports. He was quickly integrated into the school's running team and was also introduced into the football team (although he was, in all honesty, never really that good.)

It was on the next inter-schools sports day that Maurice's best day arrived. He was, of course, entered for the marathon. At first he was a little taken aback to be on the track in front of so many people and it was difficult to stretch out his run while blocked in by all the other boys and girls. Little by little he began to move towards the front of the pack, but he was far from being alone.

There were three others at his level, two boys and a girl, and they seemed quite relaxed and confident. They were starting to move away from him; he was beginning to feel that he wouldn't make it, when he heard a familiar voice in his head. His perception of the outside world dimmed, he seemed to be moving in slow motion.

'What do you want Maurice, what do you deeply, deeply want?'

'For the others to like me, to respect me…to win!'

'Your payment will be what it is that you want and need.'

Suddenly he felt it, a deep, deep contact with something potent yet quiet within himself, his breathing deepened, steadied, found its own powerful rhythm. His body took on a life of its own, he was part of, but yet separate from, himself – he flowed forward. And with the same interested detachment that he had watched the attic arrange itself, he watched himself advance towards the three lead runners. Oh no, they were mocking him again, in the distance he heard them, as always, 'Ket-tle! Ket-tle!' He started to sweat, to feel unwell, to lose his flow, but then it clicked. No, no, no – there weren't *mocking* him they were *cheering* for him; the whole school it seemed were on their feet, 'Ket-tle, Ket-tle, ruuun, ruuun, ruuun!'

And he ran – how he ran! – every runner that he had ever read about inhabited his soul, every thought, every experience, every trick was his to draw on. What's more, every moment of not being good enough, not being accepted spurned him on. Now he no longer ran, but flew. The others flowed back passed him, disappearing into his failed past. Now there was no-one, only success and acceptance.

As he arrived at the finish, the jubilant roar of his erstwhile tormentors in his ears, he closed his eyes in pleasure and relief, and the ugly, old face wrinkled up with a smile.

1.2
Margaret has taken up astrology. Her first challenge was to overcome her fear of maths (her worst school subject), but she was very motivated and her teacher was accustomed to teaching this type of student.

Next, she opened up her appreciation of world geography. And finally she plunged deeper and deeper into the study of personal psychology, discovering intellectual capacities that no-one, especially herself, would ever have imagined that she possessed.

2.2
Carl is different; he has left his hair grow, he wears comfortable jeans and, although not at all rude, he is much more relaxed in the way that he interacts with me.

He explains that he has just had another conflict with his father because he has come to the conclusion that he doesn't want to do any apprenticeship and that he has always wanted to act.

Now he has to convince his parents to support him in this...

3.2

When I stopped panicking I reminded myself of the Chinese proverb, 'a thousand mile journey starts with taking the first step.'

I took one strand of the programme and followed it as far as I could. When I got stuck, I then began another, and so on and so on. By following various strands I began to see the logic of the structure of the programme and even where some of the errors had crept in.

After I had finished the short-term data entry job, I was kept on in the hope that I could sort out the programme and make it function. I continued with it, and within a relatively short time it was up and working.

They might even still be using it this very day.

Discussion:

Many of us feel at one time or another that we are useless, incapable, incompetent, good for nothing. Some of us feel like that for most of our lives!

We are all good for something; we all have value and talents; we are all somehow, somewhere special for someone or something.

The old witch knew that Maurice could fulfil his dreams and reach his goals; he just had to reach into himself to find out what they really were and then allow those desires to find their owns means of being satisfied.

Deep within ourselves, sometimes very deeply hidden, are the abilities and traits needed to experience and live this potent, positive potential.

4: Images

1.1
Mike is 25; he has big, blue eyes and unkempt, dirty blond hair. His rumpled clothes hang badly from his skinny body.

Mike is living with some 'friends,' a Christian couple who have taken him in and taken him on as he is not capable of living alone.

It seems that he has a whole mess of emotional and intellectual difficulties that block him from any form of independence.

2.1
Solly is a nice guy; quiet, unassuming, a little timid, a little nervous. He clasps and unclasps his hands as he talks to me, his big doe eyes plead with me to find a magic solution for his problem.

For you see, Solly has never been a major wage earner for his family; his wife, the strong and dynamic Beatrice, has always carried the family.
She had risen from humble secretary to directorial assistant, while Solly had the questionable 'honour' of being one of the first 'home fathers.'

Solly says, 'Beatrice might be going blind; the stress and strain of her work, all the responsibilities and hours in front of computer screens have seriously affected her eyesight. Her doctor has strongly suggested that she should stop working altogether, at least for a year or two.

'I haven't worked for years. I don't have it in me to get a good job.'

I totally reassure him that he has more inside him than anyone could ever imagine.

3.1

I am in my thirties. I am visibly unfit and overweight. My partner and I have opened our house as a home for homeless young adults. We are doing some work in the back garden.

There is a large pile of house bricks to move, and the 'boys' are complaining that it is taking a long time to move them.

I remark that carrying six bricks at a time is hardly efficient, so they challenge me to a contest...

Images

From Tales Of Peter The Pixie

It was a day like many other days when Peter arrived at Elli's house. The sun was shining, the birds were singing and a white, powdery frosting was noticeable on Elli's small upturned nose.

'Hello Peter.'
'Hello Elli, what are you baking?'
'Apple and blackberry,' she replied, returning to the kitchen to put the kettle on and continue with making her pies.
'What are you doing this morning?' Peter stopped to think for a moment, for although this wasn't a complicated question, it was one he hadn't a ready answer for.
'Oh, I know, I'd thought I'd come round and see you.' Elli shook her head to herself and continued with the pies.

Pretty soon the tea was ready and the pies were in the oven. The two friends sat in Elli's pretty, pink and green sitting room drinking a refreshing cup of elderberry tea.
'... Yes, it really is a lovely day,' Elli finished saying, agreeing with Peter.
'What are you going to do after you've finished making the pies?'
'Well I do have some cleaning and tidying up to do. Did you have something in mind?'
'I just thought since it is such a wonderful day, maybe we could go for a walk and have a picnic.'
'Peter, that is a most charming idea, and we can have a fresh slice of pie to take with us.'

And with that they fell into discussion about the details of the picnic. Peter was to go home, via Timothy's hole, and see if Timothy would like to join them. Then he would make some sandwiches and meet up with Elli at noon, and from there they would set off for a nice walk and a picnic.

'Hello Timothy,' called out Peter. He was standing by the battered, rotten log that marked the entrance to Timothy's hole. 'Oh, 'oo's that? Wait a minute.' And from out his hole the grisly, old toad appeared.

'Oh, 'ello Peter, it's you, is it?' Timothy didn't seem very awake somehow, he kept stopping and looking around is if he'd lost or forgotten something, and then quite suddenly would start talking again.

'Good morning Peter, and how are you today?'

'I'm very well, thank you, Timothy. Are you all right?'

'What? Me? Oh yes, well actually, umm maybe…no.'

'What's wrong?' Peter was starting to feel quite concerned, he knew that Timothy was very old, but whether this was something that usually happened to old toads, or if it was something else, he had no idea.

'Wrong? What do you mean, "what's wrong?" Oh yes, I see. Well, it's a flu I think, yes, yes it's the flu.' Although Peter didn't know much about flus; what he did know was that they were curable, and he also knew someone who would know all about how to cure them.

'Elli and I are going on a picnic this afternoon. Would you like to come with us? And maybe Elli can find something to help cure your flu.'

'That is a crackin' good idea, yes, yes, yes …' and he continued to mumble to himself as Peter waved goodbye to him and returned to his own little house.

It was just after noon when Peter and Timothy arrived back at Elli's pretty, rose-covered house.

'Timothy's got the flu,' burst out Peter, just as soon as they were through the front door.

'Well,' replied Elli, 'we'll have to do something about that, won't we?' she said in her semi-serious nurse-like voice.

'Do you know 'ow t' cure toad flu?'

'Fairies know all about healing, don't they Elli?'

'Fairies know a lot about many things,' replied Elli, a little mysteriously. 'Do you feel well enough to come on the picnic?

'What?' Timothy had drifted off again.

'ARE...YOU...WELL...ENOUGH...TO...GO...
ON...THE...PICNIC?'

'I am neither stupid or deaf, thank you, Peter. Of course I'm well enough to go on the picnic.'

'Good, I can collect some herbs on the way, and brew you up a tincture when we stop for tea.' And with that decided, they set off for the picnic.

It was a beautiful afternoon, and apart from having to remind Timothy that walking involved moving his feet from time to time (as he sometimes just stopped because he forgot what he was doing), it was quite perfect.

On occasion, Elli would disappear off to find a certain herb or flower for Timothy's flu remedy. It was wonderful to have such a clever and caring friend as the pretty, little fairy.

They had decided to picnic by the side of the great gorge, a magnificent canyon, carved out by thousands of years of rivers passing through it.

'Look at me!' shouted Peter, as he balanced by the very edge of the drop.

'Peter, come away from there right now!'

Just 'cuz she's older than me, doesn't make her my mother,' was Peter's first thought, but then again, it *was* quite a steep fall if he should slip. So he shrugged his shoulders and walked back towards his friends.

'Peter, could you fetch some twigs for a fire while I go and get some water, please?'

'Okay,' and off he went. Elli took a jug out of her bag and went for the water. They both forgot about Timothy until…

'Oh 'elp!!!'

Peter was the first to arrive.

'Elli, quick! Timothy's fallen over the cliff!' Timothy must have forgotten about being close to the edge of the gorge, and just walked over. He was now clinging onto a small shrub, several feet below Peter and Elli.

'What shall we do, Elli?' The fairy stopped and thought for a moment.

'Your trousers, take off your trousers.'

'But they're the special ones you made me.' (Elli had made Peter a very special pair of trousers, made from leaves that had been super-strengthened by a secret process.)

'Hurry up Peter!' He reluctantly took his trousers off. Elli tied the ends of the legs together and passed them down to Timothy.

'Here, Timothy, grab onto these.'

'What?' said Timothy, who had gone funny again.

'Timothy, grab onto my trousers!'

'But I'm too heavy for you to pull up.'

'Please Timothy, grab hold of them.'

'No, I'd just pull you both down as well.'

'Timothy, *do as you're told!*' Now, Elli did shout at Peter once in a while, but Peter had never heard her speak to Timothy like this.

'Okay then.' And with that he let go of the bush with one of his hands, and hooked it through the trousers.

'Okay Peter, let's pull him up.' Peter was a little confused as he knew that he wasn't strong enough to pull up Timothy, but Elli seemed so sure of herself that he didn't feel he could argue. 'Okay then Peter,' he muttered to himself, 'it's all up to you now.' And with that he started to pull.

And as he started to pull, Elli, who was holding on to Peter from behind with her arms around his waist, unfurled her wings and started to slowly, but firmly, flex them. He could feel the air being gripped and forced below these thin, yet powerful silken petals.

Her fine, smooth jaw was set in clear determination; tiny delicate muscles tensed and flexed, and Timothy started to feel himself being dragged up back to the edge of the cliff.

Peter and Elli pulled, further and further away from the edge they backed. Elli's wings kept their steady, slow rhythmic beat. Peter could feel the magical power radiating from the little being behind his back. And somewhere, even when he was concentrating so hard on pulling his old friend to safety, he had time to be amazed that the gentle, little, caring, creative female that he thought he knew could be so very, very strong.

And then it was over. Timothy was safe and once more Elli was being the nursing healer.

Nothing more was said about the rescue. Timothy didn't remember, and Elli didn't mention it, but as for Peter, the sight of Elli dragging Timothy up almost by herself is an image he will always remember – that, and Elli with flour on her nose on a baking day.

1.2
Mike has a friend that is an alcoholic, last week after leaving my office he went to visit him…

'I found him in a very poor state; he had been drinking solidly for 2 or 3 days, hadn't eaten and he and his apartment were in a total mess. I pushed him into the shower and ran out to buy some food, which I then cooked and served him. While he was eating, I quickly cleaned and tidied up the apartment.
'I then phoned a centre for alcoholic abuse and made an emergency appointment. We took a taxi there and I described his case during the admission interview. The admissions assistant asked if I was a social worker, but I explained that I was just a friend.
'I phoned yesterday, he seems to be doing okay.'
[N.B.: This case history passed exactly like this, only the name has been changed].

2.2
Solly has just left my office after dropping in to see me for a closing interview.
He is still quiet and unassuming but now neither timid nor nervous.
The only clasping and unclasping of his hands is the firm handshake at the beginning and end of the interview.

Solly is now a commercial traveller. In a world where only the tough survive, Solly is the exception to the rule. His relaxed, calm, easy manner puts the clients at their ease, and he is very successful.

Everyone is honestly surprised but no-one more than Solly himself.

3.2

They are young, strong and fairly fit 16-18 year olds and they manage to carry, at their best, 12 house bricks.

I have something to prove – I manage 22!

What they could not know is that for years and years I had been helping my father in his record businesses, carrying up to 400 LP records at a time. This carrying capacity had not yet totally faded away.

Discussion:

We are more than we seem. Maybe even much more than we are aware. Often we can give an image of ourselves to others and to our own selves that we are soft, weak, incapable, rigid, aggressive, etc., etc.

The images that we live with, as with the roles that we seem forced to play, are not all of who we are; in fact they might not be who we are at all.

When the moment comes, give yourself the freedom to be different; be that self that is the most appropriate, wonderful, successful.

People might just end up with a slightly different image of you

5: Returning to Rondo

1.1

It is a winter's Wednesday afternoon and Sally arrives as usual 30 minutes in advance of her session.

Sally is 45, a part-time primary school teacher; her thick black hair is tightly pinned back in a bun. She wears no make-up and she still shows signs of nervousness and depression.

It has been over two years now since Mark was thrown off and killed, while cycling home, by a drunken adolescent driver, and Sally is slowly putting her life back together after the death of her husband. I think that it is maybe time that she thought about dating again.

'Oh no, of course not. I could never find another man like Mark, he was so kind and soft and gentle. I would be a fool to expect to find another man like him, and anyway, I'm not 20 any longer. [The age she was when they had started dating.]
'Men of my age are either sick or just want sex…'

I persevere just the same.

2.1

Sam has been on Invalidity Assurance Benefits for seven years now; she suffers from a food disorder which is now coming more and more under control.

We discuss her poor self-image and chronic de-valorisation of her by her parents, brother and sisters; how she had started university studies but was mocked on a daily basis by her father until she gave them up.

'Why don't you try again?' I ask.

'Firstly, I'm too old, [33]; secondly, it's been so long that I've forgotten how to study; thirdly, I don't know if I'm really capable and finally, what would be the point anyway?'

I remind her of my own history of restarting studies at 38, in French, 15 years after finishing my first degree.
'Anyway,' I conclude, 'what else better do you have to do for the moment? I would consider it as therapeutic.'

'I'll think about it.'

3.1
I am unemployed, living in a caravan, an associate member of the Findhorn Community.

The woman of my dreams is phoning me from Switzerland: 'I have managed to find some cheap tickets to India and I've also managed to get together enough money to pay for them.'

India was a land that I had heard of, but never thought I would ever have the opportunity to visit, and now I am being offered the chance of a lifetime.

'…You just have to find the money for your flights to and from Switzerland.'

The dream crashes at 100 mile per hour against the brick wall of a very hard reality.
I feel hurt and anger; how the hell am I going to find the money for that, and just in a few weeks?

Returning to Rondo

In a far off land, long ago, in the village of Rondo, there lived a young man, not the most handsome of lads, a bit too tall, with long, spindly arms and legs; nor the most intelligent of beings either, quite naive. Everyone called him 'The Bean' for being long and thin and green. Although it was not unheard of to make fun of 'The Bean,' he was well liked by the people of his village, for he was kind and honest, gentle and trustworthy.

And he loved the baker's daughter. Being a baker's daughter, not surprisingly, she was a little on the stout side, happy, easy-going, loving, maternal, but large and also maybe a little simple. They made a strange looking couple, but as they both had their qualities, the village folk thought they were an excellent match for each other. There was no clear moment when the couple became engaged, but just the same, it was decided that they would wed at the spring equinox. And so it was to be.

Now, there was something even more unusual about 'The Bean' that made him very special in his village, not to say in the whole kingdom. It was that he also had family in the neighbouring kingdom, to the South. For his father was a minstrel and took to travelling, following his inner guide, which sent him many a mile, even to this far-off place. It was there that he met and fell in love with his future wife, but when he disappeared on one of his travels, it was decided that the young mother should come and live with the dead husband's family, as was the custom.

Some say that it was his 'foreign blood' that made him so different and strange, although those who had met travellers from that kingdom had reported no specific differences that they had noticed. Anyway, once the future wedding had become a fact, he felt it his duty to go and inform his 'distant' relatives, those whose existence he knew of, and surely many that he didn't know of, that he was to be married to the baker's daughter.

So, as soon as the snow started to melt, and the mountain passes separating the two kingdoms became clear enough, he started off on his journey to the south, to remake contact with those parts of his history that he had not contacted for quite some time. (One must admit that he wasn't totally sure that all the parties of this group would be positive or that contacting them would be pleasurable for him, but just the same, he knew that this was the right thing to do.)

And so he set off. The path was not always that simple, but after the mountain pass, as he began to descend, he found the going more and more to his liking. This was new territory for him, yet somehow also quite familiar; it felt right, proper, important to return, to return to his own history, to his roots.

Down and down he went, deeper and deeper into this foreign country that was also his home. How he could feel so profoundly connected to something he had only the vaguest knowledge of (he surely could not remember), was a mystery to him, but he felt it just the same.

Sometime later he arrived at his destination, and he contacted those parts of his family, one could even go as far saying re-contacting parts of himself. His family was numerous and diverse.

His grandfather was dry and serious and asked of his future wife, 'Can she cook, is she strong?' His grandmother, tender and caring: 'Will she make a good mother?' One uncle, a very upright person, wanted to know if he himself was ready to take on the responsibility of being a husband and father. A very practical soul asked where they would live. 'Do you love each other?' inquired a romantic. 'Why are you worrying?' one optimist questioned. 'Are you worrying enough?' countered his pessimistic twin. And so on and so forth.

The questions, concerns and advice were of all sorts and types, but what was wonderful was that no matter how positive or negative, constructive or romantic, serious or irresponsible they were, the young man felt loved and cared for by his family.

Each reaction was somehow, somewhere for his own good. If one made him feel confident and sure while another made him question his choice, so be it; both opinions were given so as to help him advance along his path. He even, after a while, began to see how he could benefit from the negative points of view, for they showed him what to be aware of, what he would need to watch out for, how not to fail.

And so the time passed. He had felt immediately very comfortable and at home, with almost all of his family (there were admittedly some parts that were not initially totally friendly towards him: '

Why have you not contacted us before?' 'We missed you, didn't you miss us?' 'You abandoned us' etc.) and would have liked to stay longer, but somewhere he knew that it was time to start back. Then they heard the news; his kingdom had been invaded by the kingdom from the North!

The kingdoms had lived in peace for many years now, and had no armies to speak of, but in the North, for the past few years, the harvests had been very poor and the people had gone hungry.

This made for more and more unrest. And as the kingdoms had little or no communication with each other, this northern kingdom had no-one to ask for aid, and as its own resources began to run out, there was no-where left to go for help.

After one more bad harvest, the king had decided that the only course of action was to invade the southern kingdom on his border, and as soon as the snows allowed, this is what he did. Even with his small, ill-equipped army, the other kingdom was soon overrun, the borders closed and the people put under martial rule.

The young man's reaction was immediate: 'I must go back at once.' Most of his family tried to dissuade him, but he was adamant, his love was there, and so there he must be.

'I don't know how I will manage, but I trust that if I'm doing the right thing, then it must work out somehow.' He thanked his family, packed his horse and made ready to leave.
'Would you like for some of us to accompany you?' asked one of his family.

'I would appreciate all the help that I can get,' replied the young man smiling, 'but I don't expect anything of anyone. If there is some support, all the better, but I've decided that I will not look back to see if there is or is not anyone behind me, I have decided to go, whatever resources I take back with me from here will be an extra.

And with so saying, he smiled at everyone, waved, mounted the horse which had been generously offered to him, and set off home to find his loved one.

And so he started off home without a backward glance. He did not know if he was accompanied or not; if someone tried to ride beside him, he bid them retreat.
He did not want to count on others to keep up his resolve. It was not to be on account of outside support that he would undertake to return, but only through his own internal resolve.

He encountered many people along the route. Some called him foolish, others thought him a hero, all were interested that he had decided to continue. 'How can you expect to pass through the border, it's closed off, there must 50 soldiers controlling it?' 'Do you really think that you can arrive at your home village?' 'Do you realise that you might be killed?' The young man smiled gently at each interlocutor. 'I feel that it's the right thing for me to do. Something in me feels that the means to be successful are building up so that I will succeed. I am trusting this feeling.' And somewhere, somehow his words convinced those that had the means to hear.

Several days passed before he climbed the mountain pass. It seemed that much had changed for and in him in the short time since he had descended into this other, different place, since he had contacted his near and far kin. Someone stronger, surer, clearer, was returning to his normal life.

The contacts that he had made were and remained real and powerful. How was he to pass the border, to face maybe as many as fifty soldiers, just like that?

He couldn't know, but somewhere he was certain that he had the resources necessary.

So it was that he arrived at the border of his own kingdom. He could vaguely see the soldiers from some distance away.

First only a few, then more and more, until the whole troop was plainly visible. 'They must be surprised to see anyone at all, to make such a fuss for one single traveller,' he thought to himself.

What was more surprising however was that as he continued to advance, all of a sudden a great cloud of smoke appeared from the camp, which when it cleared, revealed a great emptiness; the soldiers had left, each and every one of them.

It was at that moment that the young man decided to turn and take a look behind. At first it was hard to grasp, but after a short moment he could only accept that what his eyes were showing him.

He was heading a vast army of maybe two or three hundred men and women. At the front were many members of his own family, foremost his old grandfather, but behind his proper family were scores and scores of people, some that he had never even contacted directly. Each person had their own network of family, friends and contacts – a resource of enormous potential.

Without ever having to directly confront the invading army, the young man and his followers continued unopposed on his route, gaining more and more power, as men and women of his own land joined up with this peaceful yet impressively powerful wave of humanity.

The northern army soon heard of this increasingly impressive opposing force and, not having the will to have a real war, departed at full gallop, only leaving a sad delegation to plead for some support for their beleaguered population.

(As there had in fact been no blood shed during the entire 'invasion,' the king generously agreed to do what he could to help his 'hungry neighbour.').

And as for our young man, well, needless to say, he had a splendid wedding, but when asked what his greatest wedding present was, he would modestly reply, 'Having the luck to be involved with the bringing of the three countries together.'

And as for his feat of gathering the huge army for that, 'I just trusted the forces that were already there, and directed them towards a worthwhile goal.' And with that, he would turn away, if anything, a little embarrassed to be having so much attention.

After all, he only did what he felt that he had to, and could do – only that.

1.2

It is summer, a Wednesday and Sally is late!

She swans in ten minutes after the hour.

'So sorry, I forgot the time, we were having lunch.'

Being late is not the only change; Sally is happy, relaxed, confident. Her thick black hair drapes majestically over her shoulders and down her back, her make-up is discrete but present, all signs of nervousness and depression have disappeared.

The last months have not been without incident or concerns but this is a 'happy ever after' moment and she is fully living the dream.

2.2

Sam has now finished both her first degree, (BSc) and her Masters degree a straight-'A' student.

It took her two years as an *auditrice* (un-enrolled student) to find the confidence to take the plunge and enrol. She feared that she lacked the intellectual resources to face the challenge but in reality they had just been waiting (for years and years and years) just for the opportunity to show themselves and make true a seemingly impossible dream.

3.2

Something magic happens. In the space of just a few seconds the anger and panic subsides. I feel calm, serene and maybe a little crazy. I also feel trust: 'Okay, this is challenge; I'm sure that the money will come.'

'You are a fool,' I tell myself. However, in reality I don't have any choice; either I trust that I will succeed or I renounce the entire project.

I take out my old psychic reading cards and make myself a sign. 'Readings by donation to finance a trip to India.'
Needless to say, I succeeded largely to finance the trip through the wonderful generosity of the Findhorn Community people, even a bus ticket down to London.
I just had to ask and to open myself to receive.

Discussion:

Are you a 'Bean'?

Could you be so naïve so as to turn your back on safety and good sense and trust that what you deeply know to be right will bring you power to overcome impossible odds?

Could you gather for yourself an immense army of support which, without having to beg or plead or persuade or be beholden to anyone, you could have at your back?

Could you give yourself so totally to a love, a mission, an ideal that the very thought of not giving all that you have to fulfil that thing is not even imaginable?

Could you be so desirous to go forward that you wouldn't look back, not even once?

We know that the answer is yes.

When the time comes...Just do it.

6: The Storm

1.1

Kate is 42, a middle-school history teacher. She has had to face many loses throughout her life. The deaths of her father, husband and brother, but none have ever been fully dealt with. Her mother is dying, and Kate cannot cope with losing the last member of her immediate family.

We start working on the simple concept that she herself has a future.
Kate's mother takes a turn for the worse; Kate's whole world suddenly seems to be falling to pieces.

2.1

Dave is slightly nervous. This is not unusual; he has an anxiety disorder. He is a 27-year-old accountant, very tidy in his appearance, small and dark.
He finds it difficult to be in enclosed spaces from which he cannot easily leave; public transport is of course a problem, but so are night clubs, business meetings and even the cinema.
He hasn't been to the cinema in years.

When I invoke any of these situations he starts to sweat, his heart speeds up, he fears that he is losing control.

3.1

Too much is too much! I have just received an enormous tax bill that I have not anticipated, my baby son is again sick with a heavy cold and an ear infection, Mona is giving a conference next week, I have a patient not doing well at all and I am weeks behind with my paperwork, which is piling up all over my office…

The Storm

Let your mind and your imagination take you to a place,
A place outside
A mountain, a valley, on land or water or ice or sand,
Hot or cold, north or south or east or west,
A place known or unknown,
Close or far.

There is a storm,
The sky is full black with clouds,
Thunder rings in your ears,
Lightning shocks the eyes,
The rain soaks clothes and skin,
The wind blows,
Whipping all into a terrible torment.

Your breath is short, shallow, staccato, insufficient;
Fear, anguish and panic threaten to invade your soul;
All is movement, flowing, flying, falling, fatal thoughts

The only wish is run, and to hide,
To shelter from the awful storm,
From the heavy, cold, enormous droplets of rain
Ejected from the angry sky,
Accelerating towards the defenceless earth
Only to explode, violently on and around you

Go, go find your shelter;
It exists, it is close;
Allow yourself to discover this safe place,
A place where you can protect yourself from this dangerous,
mad weather

Here, here you are,
This is it;
A moment of calm,
To catch your breath
Of respite,
To relax a little

Look around yourself,
Notice the storm,
The dark, thunder, lightning, rain
The rain, the rain that maybe seems to be a little less strong,
And the lightning, a little further off,
The thunder, slower coming, softer

Yes, yes the rain is becoming less strong, smaller, lighter,
gentler,
And the lightning is moving further and further off
And the thunder, the thunder, it is where, where, wait, wait, yes,
fading off

And look, look around you; don't you see a change in the
quality of the light?
Yes, there is something – a little more light;
We can start to see the shapes of things around us,
Yes, it is becoming lighter,
The clouds must be changing;
The solid black, heavy blanket is showing signs of age
Less solid, patches of grey

The tension of the storm has passed,
The air feels more relaxed, more calm,
The wind has dropped,

The rain is stopping,
The earth has been washed clean;
All the sad rain that has needed to fall has now fallen,
The old dry scars of the earth have been softened and healed,

The wind has cried out its pain;
It is time for a new beginning.

The light increases,
The clouds find edges of white,
And through the white, one begins to see between
Through the thinnest cracks of white appears the blue

The rain has stopped,

The wind calmed,
The day exhales all tension;
It is safe to leave your shelter

The world feels fresh and wholesome;
The warmth of a playful breeze
Somewhere dances the trees

Maybe there is grass, flowers, small animals,
Or not.

Maybe there is water close by,
Or not

The sky parts the clouds,
Which, embarrassed to have covered so much space for so long a time,
Begin to melt away;
The worn, depressed, off-white fabric
Shrinks into small islands of discomfort,
Only to vaporise as the warm, gentle optimistic sun
Beams its friendly face towards us.

Now, now it is time to totally relax,
To absorb all that is available,
To cleanse and recharge ourselves,
Safe in the comforting presence of this powerful protector;
All is deeply peaceful,
A timeless tranquillity floats on the air;

Here we can allow ourselves to release all of our barriers,
Contact the deepest, most fragile parts of ourselves,
Those parts which also count as important resources,

With whose help
We are able
To face

All that we need to face;
Each challenge, each problem, each worry or anguish,
With strength, determination, creativity, joy and humour;
Each difficult moment has its response
Somewhere, deep within us all;
We can contact the appropriate resource

And now, ready, we return, prepared for anything that life has to offer.

1.2
Kate returns to the office the following week.
Something important has changed within her.
Although her mother's condition has improved and is now stable, Kate has faced the fear of her mother's death, directly 'in the face.'
The work done on the concept that she has a future suddenly kicked in and it became real for her that her mother's death in no way was her own death sentence, rather the possibility of re-birth.

2.2
Dave participates in a regular auto-hypnosis group which I start each week with a version of the storm.
After last week's session, he managed to go to the cinema *and* to stay all the way through until the end of the film.
Well done, Dave!

3.2
Giving the auto-hypnosis session calms me down. I return to my office and focus on tidying up as the number one priority.
This, of course, does nothing to resolve my many stresses, but now I can stop spinning like a crazy top and start to face them quietly and efficiently.

Discussion:

This induction was created for a group of auto-hypnosis for people suffering from stress, panic and anxiety, and it was always the first induction that we used (with variations) every week. The message is simple; the world can feel like it is becoming totally dangerous and out of control, the storm is everywhere.

Take a moment, take distance, take shelter. *Watch* the storm; notice how you can find the way that it is not taking you anymore. Somehow, often, it is partly our own energy that (co-creates) our problems. As we allow things to happen with that certain detachment, they often just fade away by themselves.

Also, by taking time out and catching our emotional breath, so to speak, we can re-connect with our own inner resources, which are just what we have needed all along to resolve that specific problem.

As often is the case, the simple solution is…just… *relax.*

7: The Volcano

1.1

It is a Tuesday morning. A young man enters my office; he is tall, handsome, forceful looking.

He waits politely until I invite him to sit down. He is quietly dressed, reserved, even a little timid in his manner. I glance down at his entry notes; nineteen years old, half-Italian, about to start a CFC (professional training) in a large bookstore in Lausanne.

He explains his situation:

My father comes from a small town in the south of Italy, he met my mother when he came to Switzerland to find work. They fell in love and got married. I don't know if he began hitting her before I was born, but as long as I can remember he would get drunk and beat her; not every day, not even every week, but still, often enough.

She tried to protect me as well as she could but as I got older I tried more and more to stop my father so, of course, I would get it too.

By the time I reached fifteen, I was as tall as he was. At sixteen I beat him up good and he left home. He now lives with another woman and has a son with her.

He says that he has stopped drinking and that he is sorry for what he did. I don't speak to him, but I have a little sister of seven and she sees him regularly.

I now have a girl friend with who I sort of live with. Sometimes I just start to get angry, something just boils up within me and I kind of explode…

2.1

Shanti is twenty-eight years old. She comes from the north of India; she is very small and slim with exquisitely fine features. She is wearing a very smart trouser-suit.

All would be perfect if it wasn't for her red-rimmed eyes and hang-dog expression. She says:

I come from a comfortable, well off family in my region, and I wanted to finish my business studies here in Switzerland. During my studies I found an international company with which I was able to do my six-month work experience.

After I had finished my diploma, they organised a work permit for me, took me on full time and I have worked for them ever since. It is a very demanding job but I am good at what I do and I am well liked by my management team. Last year the head office in America had a big restructuring and all the top management were changed,; they have now severely cut my department's budget, but expect even more productivity. The direct management is very sympathetic, but the site director keeps making me promises that he never keeps.

I am not coping any more. My emotions keep bubbling up and then they explode into tears. I cry almost all the time…

3.1

I am five years old; my brother Lloyd is seven. He is sitting on top of me, teaching me about fighting. He is twisting my arm behind my back, hurting me, hurting me a lot.

Suddenly something breaks. I feel a huge rage within me, everything becomes a whirl, a force erupts and I find myself sitting on top of him, punching him, he screams for me to stop…

I am now twenty-eight years old. I am having a screaming row with my girl friend, the rage builds up within me and I punch a hole through a door…

The rage still exists within me, it has erupted many times in my life…

The Volcano

The image of the volcano, with its direct contact with the earth's molten core and heavy rock stopper, speaks to many of us.

For one reason or other a pressure in our lives increases and increases, there seems to be no release, no appropriate outlet, no way to reduce or relax this pressure.

It becomes intolerable, unsupportable, un-manageable, impossible to cope with – and then it erupts.

The relief is immediate, sometimes total. However, quite soon after, we are faced with the consequences of our actions. The feelings are always difficult to accept; shame, guilt, humiliation, depression or even (and not so uncommonly) further feelings of anger and hate towards the person or thing that has provoked the outburst in the first place.

Strangely enough, the common feeling that always comes before these types of experiences is that of hopelessness. The person feels incapable of escaping from the situation that is causing them pain.

When the earth's plates move and the molten lava begins to flow up towards the surface, the volcano cannot just choose to uproot and move to another location. It is stuck, sitting on an increasingly uncomfortable boiling mass whose pressure will continue to mount just until the volcano cracks and the eruption follows – it has no room to manoeuvre.

Human beings are not made out of rock, they are not fixed to a stone plinth, they can move in a huge variety of ways and directions.

As with every human emotion and experience, pain is a very important message for us. It is pain that protects us from burning ourselves, cutting ourselves or staying in emotional situations that do us harm.

Feeling that we are incapable of moving away from this 'hurting' experience is awful, but in reality, rarely true!

Most frequently, the reasons that we find ourselves unwell and stuck in these unpleasant conditions are that we do not know how to release the pressure, or else we feel incapable of letting go of the benefits linked to the situation, or the inability to let go is due to the feeling that, by letting go, we are accepting that we have failed; failed the relationship, failed the job, failed the power struggle, failed the personal challenge or, most likely, some combination of the above.

When you next find yourself in a situation where you start to feel this energy building up, don't fight it! Appreciate that this force is there to be used, to be appreciated, to be channelled.

This heat is there to generate the power that you need to change the situation in which you are finding yourself, to help you overcome the obstacles to movement and transformation.

Accept change, or else eventually you could end up destroying yourself and those things of value around you.

Enjoy your energy and power!

The Volcano

Iceland is known as one of the youngest countries of the world and boasts an abundance of hot geysers, boiling mud lakes and active volcanoes.

One volcano in particular has been much in the news in the last few months; its name is Mount Felings.

Mt. Felings is a medium-sized volcano which has been very active in recent times. There have been constant rumblings from deep inside for a long time now, and not an inconsequential number of eruptions – some minor, some, much more important.

The problem is that Mt. Felings is situated quite near a centre of population. Why these people have chosen to live so close to this unpredictable and potentially very dangerous character is quite complicated and not altogether clear, but live there they do.

Geological knowledge explains that the reason that a volcano exists is because somewhere deep down there is a fault, a crack, a break in the inner surface that protects us from the boiling, white hot mass of material that exists at the core of our planet.

This weakened barrier allows the uncontrolled matter to seep towards the surface. After a certain time, the pressure or tension becomes so great that the outer shell, the face that we see, cannot contain itself any longer, and the thing explodes.

In the past, various attempts have been made to defend against these eruptions; building physical defences between the mountain and the population, re-enforcing its own 'face,' creating certain controlled explosions so as to better direct where and when it erupted, even pumping gallons of cement into it to try and force down or block the lava from breaking the surface.

Needless to say, none of these 'solutions' succeeded in solving the deeper problem.

Finally, a satisfactory solution has been found. A number of bore holes have been drilled into the side on the volcano, into some of these holes is pumped a continual flow of water. The super-heated steam that is created by the contact of the water with the boiling mass is then received from the other holes and is piped towards the town.

From there, the steam is treated in one of two ways. It is first directed towards the town's electrical generating plant, where the pipes connect with a series of standard steam turbines. Based on a calculation of approximately how much electricity needs to be generated at any one time, the engineer activates one, two or three series of turbines. The steam not used in this process is then piped off to where it re-enforces the town's centralised heating system.

The results of this experiment are impressive; since the system was introduced the town has already been able to repay eighty percent of the construction loans. And the eruptions of Mount Felings have become a historic event. From being a constant threat and menace, this volcano has become a valued and productive member of the community.

1.2

Another Tuesday morning. A young man enters my office. He is tall, handsome, forceful looking.

He waits politely until I invite him to sit down. He is quietly dressed, reserved, yet relaxed. He smiles confidently at me as he sits down.

He explains that he has agreed to talk with his father and to accept his apologies, although he still feels uncomfortable in the relationship – time will tell. His violent outbursts against his girlfriend have greatly diminished both in force and frequency and he is becoming more and more aware what she is doing to trigger his anger, he has also taken up a martial art...

2.2

Shanti is all excited,

'I did it! I did it! I have given in my letter of resignation! At first I felt a little scared, but then I started to feel very good. I have some job interviews lined up for next week, and because I've worked in Switzerland for more than five years, I can now work wherever I like. Oh – and I haven't cried a single tear since I handed in the letter.'

3.2

I feel my rage when it threatens to explode. Sometimes I still shout, and its not very pretty.

However, I now see the challenge is to not let myself 'lose it.' Letting someone else 'win' is not the failure any more, failing is allowing the situation to be stronger than my self-control.

Strangely enough, by not entering more into the conflict, I find more space for dialogue, and through this dialogue I usually finish with a solution that also satisfies me...

Discussion:

This story was created for a patient suffering from uncontrollable anger and rage and was introduced during one of his regular therapy sessions. Of course, if you are one of us that has this type of problem, or a similar difficulty in expressing your emotions in an appropriate fashion, just reading a story is not going to miraculously take all your woes away.

However, reading and continually re-reading it might well help your conscious and unconscious mind work on your situation. Thoughts, ideas and other strategies might just present themselves as interesting and worth trying. Other approaches that you have tried that have not been so far successful might now, if repeated, bear fruit.

Admitting that we might have a problem of blocked or inappropriately expressed emotions is not always easy (even only to ourselves), but it is a very common problem, especially in English-speaking populations. Work on it, work on it, work on it – it's really worthwhile.

Hint: It is never too late – in any moment, whether you're feeling an inner tension building up, or you're about to 'blow your stack,' or even if you are in the very middle or end of exploding – to do something to change your usual behaviour.

After a while your awareness and ability to react more and more appropriately will kick in sooner and sooner and sooner, and sooner, and sooner – until it all becomes just a bad memory.

8: The Warm Furry

1.1
Larry is divorced, his wife had joined a sect and her 'guru' had insisted that he either joined the sect or that she divorced him.

Somewhere, Larry is relieved by the divorce; his wife was becoming more and more distant and 'weird' over several years. However they have a 15-year-old daughter who lives with her mother.
Since the separation two years ago, the daughter has become more and more distant towards her father and their once-strong relationship and complicity has totally faded away.

'What can I do? I'm at my wits end! I've lost her!'

'Why not try just giving – not buying her anything – just giving, being there without any expectation in return? It's important that she feels loved by you, no matter what.'

'I can do that.' (In reality, he already was; he just needed to be re-enforced in his position.)

2.1
Carole and Colin have been together for more than twenty years; they have four children, a dog, a home (with a very heavy mortgage attached) and an ever-increasing couple conflict.

Each honestly feels that they are giving much, much more than the other and the truth is that they are both giving an awful lot into the family system.

Unfortunately, neither is capable of seeing, let alone acknowledging, the input of the other.

I challenge them to try the 'impossible:' One month of giving, without any expectation of receiving *anything* from the other.

'Remember, the joy is in the giving,' I quote.

They look at me very sceptically.

3.1
Spiritual communities are places where one might expect everyone to be caring, open and available.

Unfortunately, the reality is somewhat different.

We find, in general, that there are two distinct groups of people.

The visitors: Those who come for short or long visits, who are into their own personal experiences and who often need a certain amount of looking after and support.

And

The community members: Those who have often given much of their personal time helping guests and had to answer innumerable times such mundane questions as: 'How long have you lived here?' 'Why did you come?' 'What's it like..?' etc., etc.

Such community members are, after a while, forced to 'protect' themselves from the visitors by keeping the contact to a minimum outside of the organised meeting times.

The one major exception being that of chatting up the young and attractive visitors…

As an associate member, I was in rather a privileged situation; I lived and often ate outside of the community, so I was much, much more available to give attention to the guests.

I was in a moment of my life when I wanted for little (which was rather fortunate, as I *had* very little) and I was open to giving without thought of return.

The Warm Furry

Life, as most of us understand it flows in a circular motion; plants grow and die and become the fertiliser for the next generation of plants. Water is taken up from the oceans, forms clouds, turns into rain, the rain becomes rivers which are drink by humans and animals, which is then released back into nature where it then flows back into the seas and oceans. Money flows the same way; employers pay wages, which they then share with their families, which then purchase products and services, which goes to the governments and industries, which then returns to the employees, and so on and so forth.

Somewhere we are all aware that for life to flow as it must, we must give to receive. And without thinking about, we all give, much, to many, every single day of our lives.

However, we can find ourselves in situations that can lead us more and more into feeling that we have so little (time, energy, money, etc.), and that others are taking so much more than they are giving, that if we do not 'protect' ourselves then we will end up with nothing.

We then find ourselves in the vicious spiral of less; we give less, we feel less good, we receive less, (in reality maybe, subjectively – definitely), we feel that we have less, we give less …

This spiral is dangerous!

Once we allow ourselves to enter into the system, it can be very difficult to escape it. Unfortunately, many of us find ourselves being more and more trapped into this, self-created famine.

To find the perfect balance between giving and receiving is an important challenge – but fundamentally necessary for happiness and relationship health

The Warm Furry

**My version of this parable, as told by Ken Hills, former
Chaplain at Aston University
Adapted, with permission, from
The Original Warm Fuzzy Tale by Claude Steiner, Ph.D.,
Jalmar Press, 1977. Torrance, California, USA**

Once, in a far off land, somewhere lost on mountainside was a small federation. A very, very small federation; not much more than a few big towns. Maybe not very different from many other towns of that time, but what was maybe a little bit special about these towns was that, over the years, the people had grown to have an attitude of 'every one for themselves.'
Not that they were particularly aggressive towards each other, nor strangely, were they particularly mean or greedy. They even had charitable institutions; orphanages, hospitals, churches, to which they all willingly contributed. No, it was much more subtle than that.

Maybe it was some sort of variation of a long lost tribal or clan attitude, created and nourished in a time before these extended families joined into village groups that finally grow so big that even these villages lost their independence and transformed into the communities and areas of the towns. Also, the people were all very 'correct' with each other; social, financial and political rules were all clearly defined, and justice and politeness were considered as virtues of the highest order.

Of course, not all the citizens were the same, and there was a marked difference between the populations to the extreme east and west of the federation.

The westerners were the most individualistic, the most correct and they had a total aversion to any form of debt. Financial credit didn't exist. People only took what they could afford to pay for in any given moment. Even close members of the same family kept careful records of their interactions to be sure that a strict balance of equality was kept to.

Notwithstanding this, they were not at all mean; the wealthy offered each other expensive presents and shared their luxuries with their children and friends. The value of the presents was decided in advance, and obviously the children, when they grew older, would look after their parents in the same fashion as they had been treated as children.

In the east, where conditions were the most difficult, the people still lived in little villages. Here, the energy was more 'clannish,' although they were generous enough with their 'own,' they had great difficulty giving outside this group. Their relations with the rest of the federation were based on mutual benefits of the type: 'If we control our portion of the border, and you control your portion of the border, and we agree at where these two portions meet, then we are all more safe.' Someone once described this attitude as 'positive neutrality.'

And so it was, that one winter's evening a weary traveller found himself having difficulty finding a lodging in the capital of this region. He had two important problems; first, there was an event in the town, for which all the small inns were full, and the second problem was that he had very little money. After trying for several hours all the obvious places to stay, he took to knocking on doors at random. As you might well imagine, the response of the inhabitants was a very civil, but clear, 'No.'

Despite these constant rebuttals the traveller remained friendly and polite. If he received a particularly cold response, an attentive eye might have noticed that he would fumble his hand in his right coat pocket for a moment, before again finding his positive energy.

At the very edge of town, there was an exceptionally run down, old house. The shutters were tightly closed, and neither light nor sound could be perceived from the outside. A weak tendril of smoke escaping the chimney was the only sign that anyone was living there. The traveller marched up the overgrown path and knocked on the age-worn door. For a long moment nothing happened. Then, very slowly, the door creaked open. It was very dim and smoky inside, making the small figure difficult to make out.

'What do you want?' demanded the old woman.
'Mother, it is cold and dark out here. I can't find anywhere to stay the night. All the inns are full, and none of your neighbours has space.'
'They don't have space because you haven't offered them enough to lodge you this night.'
'It is true, I have very little money to offer for my keep.' So saying so, he again felt for his fetish in his pocket, breathed in deeply, and smiled graciously at her.
'And why should I house you for nothing?'
'Why not?' he beamed back at her.

There are times in our lives when we don't really know why we do things – they just seem to be the right things to do in the moment; somehow, somewhere, we know – without knowing how or why we know, but we know. This was such a moment for the old lady, and she allowed the stranger into her very modest home.

The room was small, dark and smoky; the chimney couldn't have been swept for many, many years. It was almost impossible to make out the stranger's features; he seemed dark, but one couldn't be sure. Compared to the size of the old woman and the room, he had the air of being quite tall, but then again...

'I have already taken my supper,' she said in a defensive tone.
'Thank you, mother, for your concern, but I too have already partaken of my evening collation.'
'I have no other room than this and my own bedroom.'
'But, it is quite perfect. You are really generous to offer a perfect stranger warmth and shelter.'
'Well, goodnight then.'
'God bless you, goodnight.'

The next morning, when the old woman entered into the living room, the man was already standing by the open doorway. His coat was buttoned up to the collar, and he had his hat on, which made it difficult to make out his features.
'You won't be expecting breakfast then?'

'I have already well abused you hospitality, mother. I'm just about to take my leave. But before I go, I would very much like to give you a present.'
'I thought that you had no money.'
'This is something that cannot be exchanged for money.'
'So it is worthless! That is what you think of my hospitality?'
The stranger stroked the object in his pocket, and smiled warmly at the aged dame.
'What I want to share with you is more valuable than any object that can be bought, sold or traded.'

'What nonsense is this? I have shared my home with you, and now you want to mock me?'

'Mother, inside you, you have a tender, loving soul. Inside you are generous and caring. In spite of all you have known and learnt, you have sheltered me this night, without expectation of recompense. That warmth and humanity I have felt from you, now, you in turn can profit from.'

'Are you crazy? What are you talking about?'

'Give me your hand, mother.'

She refused for a moment, but against his smiling face, she was helpless to resist. She held out her hand Once again his hand sought the pocketed object, but this time his hand grasped it firmly, pulled it out and placed it in the old wretched hand.

Suddenly, a huge smile broke through her craggy features.

'What, what have you done? What, what is it? It's some sort of magic. I'm bewitched.'

'You are only feeling your own inner beauty.'

'But it's wonderful.'

'Yes, you are.'

'Do you have any more? How much do you sell them for?'

'But, mother, I have already told you. This cannot be sold, it can only be given in appreciation.'

'But why would anyone want to give such an object away?'

'Because that is the only way to keep it alive. If it is not shared, then it will die. It is only your own warmth of spirit that feeds it. If you act coldly, meanly, spitefully, greedily, then it will die, and you will be left with nothing.'

'But I don't understand, if I don't give it away, it'll die, but if I do give it away then I won't have anything?! I don't understand.' The stranger turned, smiling, and started to leave.

'You shall, you shall.' And he was gone.

The woman stood shaking her head, confused. Then she put her hand in her pocket and stroked the warm, furry object, and felt good and happy and content.

A short while later, there was a gentle knock on the old woman's front door. It was her grandson, who had come with her breakfast. Her youngest daughter had taken it upon herself to see that her old mother was kept alive with a daily delivery of breakfast, lunch and supper – not the richest of meals, but healthy and regular.

With the tapping on her door, the old woman felt a huge swell of love and appreciation filling her diminished body.

'Come in, come in.' The small boy was a little surprised. He was always just a little scared of this craggy old woman. What did she want now? Had he done something wrong? Was she about to scold him?

'Here,' she said, 'here is something for your mother, but you must promise me that you give it to her, and not keep it for yourself.'

'I, I promise.'

'Swear!'

'I swear.'

'Spit.' He spat. She took a deep breath, touched the warm furry one last time, felt the precious, deep inner peace, grasped it firmly, and shoved it, a little violently, into her grandson's little, shaking hand.

'Into your pocket.' Shocked, surprised, bemused, he dropped it into his pocket.

'What is it?' He stroked it gently, has heart totally open in wonder.

'It's something that she can only keep for a little while, then she has to give it away, or it will die.'

'I don't understood.'

'Just do as you are told.' And with that he ran out and headed for home.

The old woman sighed heavily. It was so wonderful – even to have held it for a short moment had been wonderful. She put her hand back into her pocket, as if repeating the gesture somehow could bring back a little of the magic, and – What???!!! It was there, *still there*, *the same*. What had happened? She was lost. How had she not given him the warm furry?

She get out her coat, tied a shawl around her hand and ventured out into the town, something she had not done these last many years. Slowly, carefully she made her way to her daughter's home. She entered to find everyone in a state of great excitement.

'Mother! Mother, you have come. Thank you, thank you! How wonderful.' It became quickly clear that each and every member of the family had received one of the miraculous objects.

'How is it possible?' She asked no-one in particular. It seemed that the supply of warm furries was not necessarily limited to just one.

'How many have you given away?' she asked her daughter.

'Oh, I don't know, maybe eight or nine.'

'Ten,' corrected her eldest daughter.

'And you still have one for yourself?'

'Of course.'

'And if you run out?'

'Then someone will give me one of theirs.'

And that's how it all started

It was of course the children who began the 'distribution.' Like some crazy game of 'pass-the-parcel,' they ran out of the house, showering each friend that they met with 'warm furries.' They raced to see who could give out most and in the shortest time. Their friends in turn gave to their parents and their own circles of friends. And so, like the morning daylight, pretty soon the whole of the capital was filled with love and warmth.

The traders from the other towns and villages each carried back their own promise of good feelings, which in turn they shared with their families and friends, and they with theirs, and so on and so on.

Hence, gently, but inexorably, the wave of goodwill towards all washed over the populace. All the desire to give, to share, to join with each other, which had lived, deeply hidden in each soul, all the goodness and joy of participating and freely exchanging with their neighbours, long time repressed, but always alive and present, was at last able to express itself freely, to be finally liberated and acknowledged to be of value.

All the positive attributes in a human being, which each of us receives as our birth right, which, although we were maybe taught to deny and suppress, stay with us, waiting patiently to be given the green light to emerge, like a golden flower, a voluptuous fruit, a singing bird, something perfect, succulent, nourishing, smooth, beautiful, warming, melodious.

All that one might see or hear as qualities in other, more wonderful, more gracious, more saintly souls; all that we could wish for or imagine as desired attributes, we have, already, perfectly formed, within ourselves.

We 'only' need to find the permission and the courage to connect to our most beautiful of resources. Yes, to express these more vulnerable sides of ourselves involves some danger, and it is possible, even likely, that we will be hurt and rebuffed from time to time, but then again, the pleasure, when it comes, makes the risks more than acceptable.

And so the joy of sharing rippled out from the capital towards the outer provinces of the republic. As noted above, all was well for a certain time, until the goodwill reached some of the more distant, more rigid regions.

In the west, the reaction was one of 'non-acceptance.' It was not that the people didn't want to receive the gift of wellbeing, only that they were totally incapable of receiving anything for which they were not able to pay for or repay the giver, even in kind, to the exact value. And as the whole system of the 'warm-furries' was that of giving without any means of repayment, it was impossible for the westerners to participate.

On the other extreme, the eastern groups readily accepted the entrance of the favoured object, and with great pleasure, distributing such to all the members of the 'tribe' within the same day. The problem came at the moment when a traveller from outside stopped to stay for a night…

'Mummy, that man looks tired and sad. I think that he doesn't have a warm furry. I'll go and share mine with him.'
'Before you so much as think of doing such a thing, you must go and ask your father.'
And so she did.
'Daddy, I want to share my warm furry with the traveller.'
'Not until I've discussed it with the elders.

You know that we have a custom not to give to foreigners.'

And so the elders met, and discussed the situation. True, there were some amongst them who argued that sharing the pleasure seemed not to diminish but to increase one's feeling of wellbeing, but those voices were few and apologetic when faced with the old ways, the customs that had served the survival of the village for centuries.

Hence, it was decided, clearly, definitely and definitively that there was always the danger of lack, of want, of famine and therefore it was an act against the group to give to an outsider.

It was a quite hard discussion, and all the council members felt sad and tired after the meeting. They each one reached to touch their comforters, but it seemed not to give much comfort, it felt less and less soft, less and less warm.

The next day, each member of the council was shocked and surprised to find that his pocket was empty! All the goodwill had disappeared, evaporated, gone. They asked of their friends and families, but as the object was passed into their hands, it immediately withered and died.

The knowledge of this so shocked and discomforted the giver, that they quickly began to refuse to give. This, in turn, weakened and destroyed their own experience of abundance, and very soon, whole towns in the east were devoid of emotional wellness. They sent out expeditions to other towns, explaining their un-wellness, and surely and certainly the malaise crept back towards the centre of the republic.

A parallel but different process was equally appearing from the west. People were beginning to ask themselves how they could possibly have the right to feel so good, so well, when they had done nothing to deserve such bounty.

And with the feelings of guilt and unworthiness they began to limit their contact with those feelings of grace and benediction, and, after a short while, they ceased to exist at all.

Strangely enough for these people, when they finally placed their hands in their pocket only to find it empty and cold, they had a deep feeling of relief. As if the world were as it should be.

True, they had lost something very special and precious, but that was normal, that vague feeling of lack and loss; this was what they had been taught was their lot - and so, again, it was.

And so it came to pass, little by little, in pretty much the same way that the circle of wellbeing had rippled out from the centre to its extremities, now, like a chilly north wind, the cold feelings of loss and lack returned, even to the first family.
'Well, daughter, what do you have to say for yourself?'

'It has gone mother – the same as with every one of us; there is no more of that goodwill left in the whole land. Even the children have lost contact with their happiness. It's no good. I kept trying to give them mine until I, too, lost hope. And now, I have nothing left either. Some people are even angry with us.

They say that we gave them hope that things could be different, that they could be well and happy with themselves and with others, only now to be disappointed – as if they never really knew what is was that they lacked – and now to have felt that and to have lost it, well, it's too much to bear.'
'And you, daughter, what do you feel?'
'Sadness, mother, to have had my chance for myself, my family, and to have lost it, it's just too sad.'

'Do you feel that you and your family deserve to feel so well?'
'What you have explained to me is that the good feelings are only my own feelings that I can contact easier by way of the warm furry. If I can feel something pleasant when I touch it, it is only because I have something positive within me. That is why, in the east, when the people started to act selfishly and to feel bad with themselves, the good feelings died.'
'So what stops you feeling good once again?'
'I had my chance, we all had our chance, and now it's too late.'
'Why? '
'What do you mean, "why?"'
'Why do you think that you only have one chance? Do you think that you learnt to walk, to talk, to read without failing many, many times?'
'And to knit!' They both broke off into fits of laughter, remembering the repeated disasters when, as a young mother, she had tried to pass on this fine art to her young daughter.
'And now?'
'And now, I knit well.' Suddenly, as a sun emerging from behind a thick cloud bank, a smile, warm and radiant, broke out from the troubled face of the young woman.

'Here,' the old woman placed something warm and furry into the trembling hand of her daughter, who grasped it in surprise and pleasure.

'But, I can feel it again, just like before!' Now it was her mother's turn to smile.

'I have an unending supply. For me, for you, it is a mother's love for her daughter, just as you have for your children. Your love for your husband is different, but also strong. The love for your family, your brothers and sisters is again different, as is the love for your uncles and aunts.

Your love for your neighbours is not the same as your love for their children, who are also loved by your own children. And still there is the soft, light love that we have for every other living person and thing.'

And so she took her new warm furry, and again returned the feelings of love and wellbeing to her own children and again the wave began.

And each time the cold waves of selfishness, loneliness, unworthiness, despair returned in the other direction, again and again she gave and gave and gave. Until, at last, they all knew, deeply, profoundly, truly, that each and every one of them had the right and the power to feel strong and well and happy and that sharing does not diminish the feelings, it re-enforces them.

And when the traveller should reach your door...

1.2

Larry is divorced, and happily so. His daughter speaks to him on the phone at least once a week and he gets to see her quite regularly.

Their relationship has evolved as is to be expected; she is growing into a young woman, but Larry is okay with that. He is just happy to have re-connected with her.

2.2

I return from a three-week break and I see Carole and Colin on my first day back.

They enter the office quietly. I look for signs to see if the induction has worked or not. I am, to be honest a little tense, four weeks was a long time to have left them, but that was just how it fell.

Coming towards the chairs they accidentally brush against each other, a faint smile crosses both their lips.
I relax, there is little more to do.

3.2

There is an attractive young woman sitting alone. She doesn't look happy. She rejects all my overtures. She has already fought off three community members trying to seduce her this morning.

I am not trying to seduce her, just to help
She continues to resist, I am persistent, she resists…

We have now been happily married for fourteen years.

Discussion:

This is such a beautiful story; full of love, sharing, trust and never giving up.

When is it best to make the effort to reach out and to give? When you feel that you have nothing!

When it seems that your pocket has nothing in it at all, dig in – *dig deep* – you'll find it. Even if it seems so sad and so poor, even if it's not enough even for yourself. Give.

We all pass through those awful times when it seems that nothing is going right, that we have less and less, that the world is a sad, cold, empty place. And worse than all that, the things that we considered important; a relationship, a job, money, health, security etc., etc. are suddenly threatened or removed.

We might feel lost, scared, depressed, empty, lonely, panicked, anxious, angry, hurt, abused, refused, unloved, unsupported, untrusting, uncared-for – or worse!

If you feel that you have nothing that can help you feel better – then give to others.

Giving creates an energy; this energy works in both ways, both the giver and the receiver benefit. Maybe it is *that* energy that you need.

Do it, do it well, keep doing it – feel warm all over.

9: The Fortress

1.1
The X family are an immigrant family from Kosovo, they are Muslim and proud of their heritage.

They are a family of five; the parents, a son of twelve and two daughters of fifteen and ten.
They have known war (although not directly), as well as loss, fear, displacement, culture shock and rejection (the Swiss are not especially open to non-nationals.)

All these experiences have resulted in a particularly close-knit family unit.

For their first few years things have worked fairly smoothly; the father has found work and the children have integrated well in school – the mother occupies herself with the house, which I understand is impeccable – Kosovar women are exceptionally house proud.

The problem now is that the children, who have had until recently very little contact with other children outside of school, now, want to spend more time with their new friends and no longer stay closed within the family system.

The father, in particular, is concerned that his children will learn 'bad habits' from the local children.

The family is now in conflict.

2.1

Gale has been hurt in relationship; she still carries the emotional scars of her rupture with Tim, after he two-timed her with a mutual friend.

She is not my patient; Tim is.

'I really don't know how it happened. Gale was so busy and stressed with her studies and Pam just happened to be always there and ready to listen to me. I didn't really two-time Gale with Pam. I only slept with Pam the one time. We'd been out drinking together and I felt so bad that I went straight to Gale and confessed to her.'

I asked if she would be willing to come to a session. Her response was that she would see me, but only if it was the two of us alone. Tim said that he was okay with that.

Gale is an attractive 22-year-old law student with fine long brown hair; tall, maybe a little on the skinny side.

'He really, really hurt me. I don't know whenever, if ever, I will trust any man again – let alone Tim.'

3.1

Coming out of one relationship and going into another is never easy.

My relationship with my ex was complicated to say the least. Needless to say, my ability to open myself to and to trust another women, deeply and fully, was sadly damaged.

I had met Mona in October, just before her birthday, and things had immediately clicked between us. After she returned to Switzerland we phoned and wrote almost every single day.

She flew over to see me or I flew to her as often and for as long as we could afford.

However there was a deep, protected part of myself that was neither open nor available.

The Fortress

There had been wars, awful wars. The invaders had done terrible things, the pain and suffering had been intense, the scars never really healed.

In defence of ever having to face the pain again, the king had ordered his people to build a massive defence, a fortress; a construction so big that it could house a complete town with all the people, trades, tradesmen, farmers and farms. In fact, they would be totally self-sufficient. The massive doors were closed and bolted, and from that day onwards, nobody ever left the fortress.

One day, a young girl by the name of Hirondelle looked out over the distant meadows, bathing in the gentle morning sunlight, populated by small animals playfully running hither and thither, enjoying the early spring day. She looked and she looked and she started to feel ever so sad.

This was far from the first time that she had felt this pang of deep pain. She had not only often felt it while gazing out on the meadow, but also while watching the other children playing from the shelter of her little home, or hidden safely away in a dark corner.

For Hirondelle, or Elle, as she was usually called, was not welcomed by the other children. As a baby she was physically badly scarred, and this made the other children uncomfortable to be with her, and so, excluded from their society she could do nothing but stand and watch from a safe distance.

It was true, that it had been some time since the rough boys had been aggressive towards her and had sent her home crying and ashamed, but just the same, there was no need to repeat the episode; the memory was still painful enough without having to experience it once again.

And so, there she stood, wistfully looking out across the unending openness.
'Oh how I wish that I could just go out and run and run and run. To feel the freedom, to breathe the fresh, pure air carried from afar. Why stay here imprisoned all my days?' And why, indeed? It was in that moment that she resolved to go outside, to open a portal between this inner, closed, protected, frightened world, and that other; outer, open, naked, confident .

To her, the idea seemed obvious, reasonable, sensible. Her parents didn't hold the same views.
'Haven't you suffered enough?' was her mother's emotional reaction.
'How can you think to put yourself – and maybe all of us – in danger?' said her father, who, being a high member of the guards, had a more practical response.

One would think that things would have ended there. The parents' disapproval, or to be more exact, total rejection of such an idea, should have been enough to discourage Elle from her desire, but she was so in need to break out of the prison that she felt herself living in that she couldn't let it drop. Day after day, night after night, she begged and pleaded and argued with her elders and betters. 'It's not safe, it's not safe, it's not safe,' was the response, time after time.

'But it's my choice. Can't I choose for myself? No-one's asking anyone else to risk anything. If I'm putting anyone in danger, it's only me.'

Eventually, with her father's reluctant support, she obtained an audience with the king. The king listened attentively to her pleading. When she had finished, he looked round at the others of the court.

'She says that she would be the only one put into any danger. As king, I wish to rule by consent, not by force. We have built this protection in which we live by our own free choice.

This was not built as a prison, and each one of my subjects is a freeman. I do not feel that I have the right to stop her, or any others from risking their life as they might see fit.'
A huge wave of emotion was flowing up Elle's body...
'However, there still remains the question of parental responsibility and authority. On that I have nothing to say, other than if I was your father, I would think very carefully before allowing you to do such a thing.'

The work to gain her parents agreement had been already well under way since she first shared her project with them; the completing of the task didn't take so long.

And so, one spring morning, a few days after the king had given his ruling, Elle made her way through the various inner and outer walls of the fortress. The short journey of only a few yards, took an extraordinary long time. Each time they came to door or a gate, the appropriate keys had to be found and the lock, long since rusted and blocked from lack of use, had to be prepared to be opened. Sometimes the lock took a considerable amount of brute force, sometimes more subtle manipulations were necessary to open it.

Sometimes the lock was relatively easy and sometimes the lock was so difficult to open that the locksmith, her father and the small group of soldiers were all ready to give up, except, of course, Elle.

After a while, they all started to get more and more excited by their progress; reaching the outside, opening the door, the last lock, became a real, possible goal. The difficult locks became a challenge, everyone putting all their efforts into solving the problems to unblock them. Blocked - unblocked, blocked – unblocked; last two obstacles; blocked – unblocked; finally the last barrier, the last locks; unblocked, unblocked, unblocked – open!

As one man, all the soldiers had hurled themselves to force open the great wooden stopper and the rusted hinges had resisted for a long moment before giving way with an almighty crack!

And they were out. The euphoria lasted but a few minutes, not long enough to leave the proximity of the walls, before Elle's father, remembering his position and responsibility, ordered the soldiers to return inside the safety of the fortress. Although they quickly responded to his orders, as they were well trained to do, it was not without a little pang of sadness that they acquiesced to his command.

Suddenly, she was alone. Her father had not even stopped to wish her luck or to take care. He was too taken with returning his men to the safe confines of the fortress. She looked carefully about her. It was just the same as she had seen from the window, but the experience – that was something else. Her heart was beating furiously; fear? excitement?

Both! Freedom, for the first time in her life she was totally free, free to run, free to shout, free to sing, free to dance, free to be herself, in any way that she might want to be.

She was about to start to move a little away from the walls when she glanced up at the window; the window where she had spent so very many hours just gazing out onto this glorious openness. There was a movement, squinting against the sunlight in her eyes. She made out the form of a woman. It was her mother. She waved to her, and the figure in the window waved back.

And then she turned, her back to the wall, and started to walk, a little slowly – after all, it was a little scary to be outside. 'Is it really so dangerous?' she asked herself, a little nervously. Trembling with excitement and fear, she started to run. By running she could cope better with her strong, mixed emotions.

She was running towards the little hillock she knew it so well. The grass there had a strange type of green colour, somehow rich and varied. The surprise was total. The reason that the grass looked so unusual was due to the huge variety of beautiful flowers that grew there.

She bathed in the new sensations, the warm breeze, caressed her damaged skin, bringing far off odours of rich, dark forests, pure, fresh mountain springs and hot, dry deserts

She danced and sang and played, no longer excluded from a world in which she couldn't participate. Here, she was queen; this was her realm, and she was free, free, free to express any and every emotion. No longer imprisoned, locked up, disallowed.

Here she could laugh and cry and scream and shout. There was no-one nor anything to restrict her contact with the real nature.

As if she had opened a huge tap, the emotions all just poured out of her.

Suddenly she heard a voice.
'Are you all right?' The soldier that had been ordered to guard the gate had heard her shouts and screams and had come running to check that she wasn't being attacked by the enemy. He arrived, sword drawn, white and shaking, and very out of breath.
'Of course I am, silly.'
'But I heard screaming.'
And it felt so, so good. Why don't you try it too?'

He looked down at the crazy child, out here where it was dangerous, suggesting that he just let go, express his deepest feelings, connect to all that he had bottled up for so long. But she looked so happy, so free, so contented. Could it be so awful to feel a little the way that she seemed to be feeling? But then again, he was a soldier, and he had his duties. Well, then again, wasn't guarding her one of his duties also? And why not benefit from being out here, so very far from every one, free to fully express all that he had repressed since entering into the fortress?

'What do I do?' The question seemed so ridiculous.
'Do what you want, what feels good.'
He re-sheathed his sword, unbuckled the belt and placed them both on the ground. He breathed in very, very deeply, clenched his fists and punched them high into the air, letting out a huge cry – a cry that was at the same time one of anger, of pain and of release.

And again; deeply, deeply in, hold, and out – touching deeper and deeper to his inner, profound being. The quality subtly changed with each breath, becoming more and more animal, primal, primitive, essential; the world both reduced and expanded. Reduced to the degree that nothing nor no-one else physically existed.

Expanded, to include an enormous all-enveloping emotional universe. He was one, one with this universe, one, one with all nature, one, one with himself.

The sun was setting, so the soldier escorted Elle back into the fortress.

The next day, Elle and the soldier, who had heartily volunteered for the job, returned to the outside. All went well until Elle's father, who had decided to check on the well-being of his daughter (and exactly why the soldier had wished so strongly to accompany her), came to the gate. It was not guarded, as the soldier was not at his post. 'What had happened?' His panic turned to cold anger when he spied his sentry lying stretched on the grass, his sword carefully sheathed, some two metres away.

'What's this?!' he roared out, but before the soldier had time to react, Elle rushed into his arms.

'Daddy, daddy, how wonderful that you have come. Isn't it wonderful? Just smell the air! Have you ever smelt anything so grand? Look, look, over there, there's a warren of rabbits that live there. And up there, in that tree, there's a blue bird, and I think that it's nesting. Oh daddy, thank you, thank you for helping me to have all this.'

And with that she jumped up into his arms and hugged him like she had never hugged him before.

She was so, so happy. He couldn't ever remember seeing her so alive, so full of excitement, so full of wonder.

He stood there, entwined within the embrace of his offspring, feeling happier than he had felt since he was a young man, in love with the woman who was to become the mother of this child.

'Stay with us daddy, stay with us.'
'But the fortress – it's undefended.'
'There's nothing out here sir,' said the soldier. 'There are too many wild animals and birds that would be disturbed by troop movements for there to be anyone moving about out here. Look sir, a doe and her little one – an army would supplement their provisions by hunting them. Deer wouldn't feel safe with humans if they'd seen others hunted down by them.'
'Please, please, daddy.'
And so he stayed, and he profited with a contact so deep and rich with himself and his daughter, that the next day he brought his wife out to share in the experience.
And she brought out her sister, and the sister brought out her family, and their children invited their friends, and the friends' parents began to venture out. And so, sooner or later, every person in the kingdom experienced the joy and the wonder that the open air could offer them; to feel at last free again, free to feel all that there was to be felt, to experience all that there was to experience, to share all that there was to share.

And so the population moved back out into the open world. One by one, each re-experienced what it was to feel the fresh air on their bodies, to feel the soft fresh grass under their feet, to feel the joy of running, shouting, laughing, even crying with total abandon.

The people had returned to themselves. And, of course, Elle; she was a heroine!

1.2

We have found a compromise:

In the first instance, the children were allowed to invite some of their friends into the family home. After the parents became comfortable with this, and they had met and spoken to these friends, they then contacted the friends' parents and then the children were allowed to also meet in the homes of these vetted friends.   Little by little, the space is opening up.

I am now awaiting the first request for the daughter to attend a disco!

2.2

It has taken six months; they must love each other because it has been a tough road for both of them.

She proudly shows me the engagement ring. She is talking a lot, he is subdued, even a little embarrassed. I wish them all the best and warn them that all relationships have their ups and downs. 'Yes, we know,' they reassure me.   I am quite reassured.

3.2

It is March. To be exact, it is the 11th of March, my birthday. I am sitting on her bed in her wonderful studio in the heart of the old city of Lausanne.

'I have bought one or two little things for your birthday,' she says and smiles at me.

She pulls out a present; a T shirt with a quote from Oscar Wilde, - 'Our follies are the only things we never regret'.

And then another carefully chosen gift...and another...and another...and another...   It is not just the quantity of the gifts, which in the moment seem unending, but the immense care and attention with which each and every one have been chosen.

I am totally overcome. The last walls that were in place to protect me melt. I am perfectly safe without any protection.

Discussion:

We all get hurt some time in life, sometimes at the very beginning, sometimes later on. Sometimes it's a little hurt, sometimes it's bigger. Sometimes we quickly recover, sometimes we don't.

Whatever your situation might be, *be careful!* The message is not to be foolish, not to just close your eyes and risk, not to put yourself back again into the same painful situations that you have experienced – don't be so foolish. If you have experienced repeated deep emotional disappointments (many more than one might consider as the norm), it is important to really ask yourself is there maybe some type of pattern; the relationship(s) of my parental figures, of people towards myself or those close to me during my childhood? Am I often a 'victim'?

If you find yourself saying yes to these types of questions, then what you need is not to re-open yourself to just any relationship but to try and work through the patterns that you have first, through, for example, counselling, self-help books and groups, friends, inner reflection…

But, if you don't fit into the above pattern of having had 'relationship problems' in a clinical sense, then just try and be aware. Is there a real, important danger that the next time that you stick your nose out of your ivory tower someone will be waiting there just to chop it off?

Go on, risk it: – Live!

10: Emptiness

1.1
Dolly is a big woman; much, much bigger than I could have guessed from the soft, polite voice on the phone.

My first concern is purely practical: 'Which chair should I offer her – or should I take a sturdier model from the waiting room?'

Dolly is only 22 years old, but could be mistaken for much older; she wears a dark, baggy track suit. It's a style that I know well from treating other patients with eating disorders; overweight, depressed, poor self-image.

Dolly's parents are of rich, Greek stock. Her father owns a profitable multinational import-export business. (He also has a serious weight problem.)

He is a 'very busy man' and has been such ever since Dolly can remember.

Dolly's mother is a socialite, always out or entertaining.
I suggest to Dolly that she has been compensating for the emotional lack of her parents' availability since early childhood.

However, she fails to appreciate my point of view and continues to criticise herself for being for being a failure – 'After all that my parents have given to me.'

2.1
Donald is aware that he has a problem; he has been in therapy for compulsive gambling, alcohol abuse and for depression, but nothing seems to be able to keep him on an even keel.

Donald remembers little about his childhood but can well imagine that his problems stem from there; he hopes that hypnosis might help.

3.1
I am four years old and I suffer from chronic nightmares. I wake up scared and feeling very alone.

I go and sit outside the door of my parents' bedroom. I don't dare to knock, let alone go inside

And so I sit, all alone, cold and shivering, hoping that one or other will come out and find me.

A coldness enters into the very centre of my little self...

Emptiness

Somewhere, deep, deep, down inside,
It haunts,
It waits,
Skulking, within the shadows;
Lurking,
Hiding,
It waits.

There are times
Of inattention,
Loneliness,
Sadness,
Disappointment,
When we might
Slip
Instantaneously,
To plunge
Immediately;
Where it waits.

Where it waits
Intentionally
To catch
Us
In its icy claws
Of empty
Despair.

And there
We are
In the
Black
Nothingness

Until
It bores of
Us,
Releases
And returns us
To normal,
Ordinary,
Daily
Existence

But our lives
Are neither
Normal nor
Ordinary.
For, like the day,
Overshadowed
By
Ever-present,
Black,
Heavy
Clouds,
That
At any moment
Could open
To release
Their cold, cold,
Penetrating
Wet.

The
Emptiness
Waits,
Stalking our every
Waking and
Sleeping moment.

With the
Ever present
Threat
Of its
Malefic
Presence.

At best
It
Numbs our
Daily pleasures

At worst
It
Invades all.

Fear and
Anguish
Are our
Workfellows
Playfellows
Bedfellows;

Waiting,
Waiting,
Waiting
For their moment to
Drag us down to
Their
Awful
Lair.

How can one
Compensate this
Constant
Threat?

Too much
Control of
Self,
Emotions
Work or
Bed or
Food?

Or maybe
Too little control of
Emotions or
Work or
Drink or
Drugs or
Bed or
Food?

The moment that the
Feeling
Begins to
Grip, we
Rush
Headlong
Into our
Compensations.

And maybe,
Just maybe, they
Succeed in the
Moment.

But
Not for long.
It will
Find
You
Again and
Drag
You
Screaming,
Silently,
Down,
Down,
Down
Into
Its
Awful
Depths.
So,
        So,
                So,
There is
Nothing then to
Do, is there
Not?

If there is
No escape
From
IT
What can one do?

'Take my hand.'
'Why, for what?'
'Trust me.'
'Why do I need to trust you?'

'So to face your fear.'
'Fear?!'

'IT.'
'!!'
'There.'
'No!'
'Then run your whole life.'
'But, I cannot.'
'Alone, no; together, yes.'
'But if it is too awful?'
'Then we stop.'
'We can stop?'
'When it is you that chooses to enter, appropriately
accompanied, you can always exit at will.'
'To start, when?'
'Whenever, now.'
'Now?'
'When-ever.'
'Now, …. how?'

'We are one.
 We
 Experience
 Together.
 Aloneness is forgotten.
 Ready?'
'Ready.'

 'The day is fine and
Bright and
Warm and
Safe.'

'Fine,   Bright,   Warm, Safe.'

'There is an entrance,
A mountain cave,
A shallow pool,
Hollow tree,
 Doorway,
A door,
Portal... ...
Enter...
Begin the descent.'

'It is getting
Cold and
Dark.
I feel fear.'

'And descend.'

'Can I stop?'

'If you wish.
 Stop now?'

'No, maybe a little deeper.'

'And it is...?

'Cold and black.
Nothingness.'

'Contact the non-existence.
Find the edge,
The surface,
Extremity,
Touch it,
Feel it,
Sense it;

Smooth, rough, wet, dry, solid, flexible.
Take your time.
Here, time is your friend.
And now,
Create
Light and warmth.

Here, the
Transformation
Begins.
And here
I must
Give place to
Your
Inner guide,
Who will
Help you to
Befriend this
Inner space, and to
Continue the
Metamorphosis,
Until this
Becomes a
Warm,
Safe,
Private space.

Stay as long as you like.
Come as often as you wish.

Happy,
Home-making.'

1.2

Despite several attempts to involve Dolly's parents in their daughter's therapy, there remained a total lack of acknowledgement that Dolly has had any reason to have suffered during her privileged childhood, nor that their presence in the therapy could bring anything useful.

However, this obvious lack of support has helped Dolly to put into question her parents' behaviour towards her and how the same lack of availability in her youth has resulted in her poor self-esteem and...her eating disorder. This awareness then turned into anger and resulted in an important family conflict; 'I deserve more, I deserve better!'

The anger has now had time to cool and to be transformed into a tough, focused attitude towards transforming her life. And, it's working!

2.2

Although hypnosis is not (as some might think) a perfect way to access past memories (because the past is always being re-created in the mind), it can connect with emotional memories, which, even if not strictly 'true,' still effect our present-day lives.

Working with Donald, we accessed a number of difficult moments of sadness and loneliness which we have dealt with.

Donald is now much, much less controlled by his compensatory behaviours.

3.2

I give up on the chance of one of my parents appearing to comfort me. I climb into my big brother Lloyd's bed.
I find warmth and comfort next to his warm, sleeping body.
Peaceful and secure, I drift back into a peaceful sleep.

Discussion:

This induction is one of my central working tools for people who have experienced a deep emotional childhood lack as well as for all types of eating disorders and for all forms of dependence, deep seated depression, as well many other more general problems.

The theory and practice is that all these cases suffer from a constant, although not necessarily conscious, feeling of deep emptiness.

However, this feeling of a cold, un-fillable, black void is something that most of us feel from time to time; when our lives seem strangely empty, when we have lost an important element (relationship, job, etc.), or most bizarrely, after having accomplished a major project.
There are also some of us that, although not 'sick' psychologically, never the less often experience a recurring sensation of some unclear dissatisfaction – a need or hunger for something that is never that which we have.

No matter what your reality is, this experience can be reparatory or 'relaxatory.' What it is *not* meant to be is a sufferance! If things start to feel too uncomfortable: *STOP!* You are not a patient in the safety of a professional's care, you are an individual having an interesting, maybe useful experience. That is all – hence: Enjoy.

11: A Good Moment

1.1
David is sweating. This is not unusual for him; after all, he is very overweight, but this is not his reason for coming to see me.

David is anguished about his future. He has always been a worrier; his mother is the same. However, his concerns for the future have become more and more invasive since his grandmother, with whom he is very close, has become ill.

2.1
Hanna looks miserable; thick, owl-size glasses, badly cut hair, poorly chosen clothes, mousiness on mousiness.
Hanna 'doesn't know who she is,' her parents are Swiss-French and Swiss-German, her grandparents and great-grandparents were Jewish and Catholic, hailing from Switzerland and various other parts of our globe.

3.1
I am stressed. This in itself is not so unusual, but at this given moment I am supposed to be on holiday.
We are staying with my wife's grandparents in their old country cottage in the Romanian countryside.
I have brought piles of research articles to sort out for my doctoral thesis – it's a lot of work!

A Good Moment

He looked at her face, hard, cold with rage.

'You've...never...loved...me!' She hurled the words, each a separate individual dart of pain and anger. He instinctively ducked, as if to avoid a real, physical attack. And although in 'reality' they were only words and emotions, he felt as though there would have been very little difference if she had picked up a handful of small, sharp objects, and had flung each, one after the other, towards his head.

There seems to be a strange part of the human condition that, when faced with a crisis where it cannot immediately find a solution to its problems, the person dissociates from the moment. The problem or danger moves momentarily to the periphery of attention, always present, of course, but, for a short instant, in a secondary position.

It's as if, when running away from a danger, we stop for a moment or two to catch our breath, and look around for a means of escape. The psyche, too, takes its breath.

His attention flowed out of the oppressively ordered room. Long gone were the days when one had the possibility to live in 'untidiness.' Each and every object not programmed as belonging to the room or placed on a 'workspace' was smoothly swallowed into the 'hold-space' after several minutes of immobility.

The dark, heavy clouds obscured the moon. It was grey and rainy, which gave an interesting effect to the night's 'sky-pub.'

All new <u>indu-bike</u>. 400 kilometres per hour. Free pair of air oxyhoods with every purchase.' An impression of great speed was induced by the stream of colours, zipping along the clouds behind the attractive message. The words melted into others. 'Thursday the 4th, 20:00, to date 2,402,358 units sold, what's you're lucky number?'

She looked small all of sudden, as if all the air had been taken out of her. Her triangular, elfin face, once so incredibly attractive to him, now looked too pointed at the chin. The powerful, dark, mysterious power, dangerously sexual, had drained itself from her fragile body. He again felt a certain tenderness for this wounded deer, this little thing, but now it was too late.

Yes, too late, she had shown him a side of herself that he just couldn't accept, a sort of demanding, possessive streak.

Of course he had loved her, in his way. He had taken her to fancy restaurants, bought her nice gifts, he had even told her that he loved her, stroking her short, curly, gold and silver metallic hair. They had made plans, common projects, joint purchases, holidays; real projects…marriage, even.
So, even if it was only a two-month provisional marriage contract that he had offered her, what could one expect? The good relations with most of his other wives hadn't lasted their contractual periods, even though he had reduced them more and more with each successive wife. What was a man to do? He wanted to be fair and honest with her. Yes, yes, he loved her, but that didn't mean that he imagined staying with her for the rest of his life; nor, to be strictly honest, for the rest of this year.

She was just being unreasonable…His awareness refocused on the faint rocking motion, the warning light…

****

She was nervous. It was to be accepted. She toked on a 'mah', again and again, the THC entered her respiratory system, she visualised the calming chemical entering into her blood stream, the oxygenation process within: The blood returning to the heart, and then being pumped, forcefully up to the brain. From there, it begins to seep through the system, and she begins to feel calmer, and calmer.

This visualisation technique was taught to her during one of her detox seminars, after one of the regular, surprise testings at work, with the idea being that the visualisation helped to greatly intensify the experience, reducing the need to take as much of the cannabis as she had the habit of doing. A feeling of anger rose from her gut, cramping her breathing, blocking itself at her throat. It was a total abuse of personal liberty to include a clause in an employment contract where the company had the right to screen any and all of its personnel for drugs at any time and to insist that they follow counselling sessions, at their own cost, if their level was over some bloody arbitrary limit.

It was no good, the mah was empty, and she still felt like hell. To break open a second one straight away would surely take her over the company limit, but it was no good, she couldn't go and face him shaking like leaf in the wind.

Aaahhh, yes, yes, that was it! Now she started to feel the relief, the gentle, soothing calming effect, reaching further and further down, deeper and deeper into her troubled psyche. Of course she could have broken open a 'coki', but for her, the reactions could be dangerous. Adding a hefty dose of unquestionable confidence to her very raw nervous system could end in a very violent exchange, not really the best mood for eating humble pie from your boss.

Her hand waved gently, palm front, before the id plate of the door, the palm reader made her hand tingle. How amusing, her lips started to twitch towards a smile. No! No, that wouldn't do, got to be serious. The door flickered red for a few moments only to fade into a welcoming green as it melted away, sliding graciously to one side.

She inhaled deeply, held the breath…three, four, five. Slowly exhale. Back straight, shoulders back, winning smile, glide in.

'Good morning, equal.' The standard greeting, painfully ridiculous. She floated on a carefully controlled outward breath.

'Good morning, equal.' His cool smile mocking the words even as he was uttering them.

There was of course no desk between them, and all the chairs were all exactly the same.

Yet, that was his chair, back to the window, facing the door and the info-wall, now politely blanked for all but the clock-calendar, Monday the 8th, 08:30, on a background of a wild pasture.

'I think that maybe you have some idea of why you have been invited to see me this morning.' His tone and manner were even and friendly, but then again, they always were, one doesn't reach his position without having spent months of training on all questions of communication – verbal, non-verbal, para- and meta-verbal.

Something in the disharmony of his modes of expression and the real message which he was about to express seemed strangely amusing to her, but somewhere there was a part of her that was still able to keep watch, and blocked the mounting emotion.

'We have been very, very appreciative of your many talents, and over these past months, you have really entered into our team. Unfortunately…it has been decided that another team composition might be more bottom line…'

…It was there that she stopped listening, she felt herself dropping down, quite quickly, the red warning light flickered…

****

'Good afternoon, this is police unit 40079 of the mid-western freeway. You are informed that the 'White-Way', transversal tunnel is experiencing a heavy traffic build up on all routes above 500 metres and will be closed off as a security measure until further notice. Your transports have therefore all been redirected to lower altitude routes. Please confirm that this re-programmation has been correctly registered and actioned.'

The voice of the police emission sounded clearly in his head. One was often a little angry with this cavalier attitude of entering deeply into someone's conscious without any consideration for the experience that they might be involved in, but on this occasion it was a very welcome interruption.

He watched as the vehicle began its gentle descent. Of course, the chance that the computer-controlled pilot wouldn't have received or actioned the police instructions were close to zero, but the rule of always having a licensed pilot ready to take over the control was still in force, even if the technology had advanced dramatically since the first land-based auto-pilots had come into use.

He closed his eyes and checked the route forecaster, only to be informed that the closure of the top two thirds of the tunnel would mean a 93.5% probability of his sitting in a 30-kilo-long traffic jam for the next two to four hours. The choices were simple: A) wait; B) find another route, which would entail a 400-kilo detour and therefore take another two to three hours of route, or C) find the nearest service stop, and try to enjoy the occasion. Since, as of yesterday, he was a single man, and the idea of an ice-cold beer was always a good one, he settled for 'C.'

****

She was not at all pleased with the news. She had an R.D.V. with 'the girls' at 21:30 chez Hacks, and she felt in desperate need to share her worries about Monday's meeting with her boss. At least there was the etherphone…

****

He was not the only one to have had the good idea of stopping and waiting for the traffic to lighten, and while hovering like some sort of ultra-patient metallic bumble bee, he took to reflecting on the interruption of his thought experience by the police, of how the first implants had been undertaken by some avant-garde adolescents so that they could be connected to their music 24/7, of how quickly the portable telephone companies had been to offer the operation free of charge in exchange for a lifetime subscription to their services and of how the implant, always improved and refined, would now have the effect of intensifying both remembered and fantasised experiences.

The deepened experience was interesting in its ability to be felt as if real; you really seemed to be there, all the senses came into play. You could be skiing, heading downwards, feeling the swaying of your body, gently to and fro, to and fro, to and fro, leaning this way and that way, down and up and down and down, as the ground undulates under you, left and right, the glare of the reflected white, so strong that your eyes wish to close all by themselves, and for just the shortest moment, you let them close; how, because it is only in your head, you can keep them closed, or not, as you wish. How you can feel the cooling breeze, the flakes of snow on your face, the sounds of others around you, to be totally taken and involved with this intense moment.

And yet, you are not asleep, you are totally aware of everything that is happening in the real world. You can hear, see, smell, touch everything that is here, only you don't really want to pay it any attention.

It only takes something of real interest to happen, someone arriving that you want to interact with or something of a dangerous nature, and immediately we are totally back and present.

His attention was re-focused by his car auto-parking on one of the upper parking bays, at last!

It would not be wrong to say that he wasn't particularly surprised to find that all the cafeterias were full to choking, but he was getting a little worried of finding anywhere to sit when he noticed a space. It was at table for four, only there were only three chairs near it; the fourth had obviously joined a larger group elsewhere.

On one of the chairs sat a small, balding, slightly overweight man. More than that it was not possible, or dare I say interesting, to know, he was busy reading his 'book.'

She was sat on a seat to the right of the man, a rather attractive thirty-something, with her jet-black hair held up at an unlikely angle by a series of magnet pins.

She looked quite tense, sitting there talking twelve to the dozen, clicking her mirrored nails on the table top. She was either totally nuts or she was talking on her ether-phone.
True, for him, at this time all women were very likely to be several degrees short of a boost, but it seemed, just the same, more than likely to be the latter. The third chair was about to be occupied by a weary, handsome debonair man about to appreciate a well-deserved beer…

The cold beer poured itself out of the synthomat, frothy, cold and slightly alcoholic. True, the name, 'Ol' Pete's Home Brew,' wouldn't pass the trade's description act, but nobody gave a damn, and it did the trick.

'…and I was just re-playing next Monday's final meeting with that worm and, as usual, the police broke in to say that we're going to be hours and hours late… Sorry, Sue, I'm getting a strong disapproving image of mum. I'd better speak to her, bye.' She pressed a small indent by the side of her temple. 'Hi, mum…yes, yes, I know…yes, but…No I don't know. Well I was just about to call when the bloody police cut in with the pile up, and you know how it is, so I forget. Got to go, Sue is just calling, bye.' She blinked her eyes, as if waking up from a dream, and looked around her.

'It's really not right how the police just barge in with their messages.' She thought for a moment before deciding whether or not to reply to the stranger that had just sat down opposite her with the beer, not bad looking, a bit grey maybe, seems more of a friendly type than a creep on the pick-up.

'Yes, it's really not good enough. Privacy and all.' He smiled encouragingly at her.

'Although,' she sighed slightly, having decided to enter into communication with him, 'they hadn't interrupted the most wonderful of experiences.' She smiled back at him, not that she was quite sure why, nor why she had volunteered such intimate information.

'You were not the only…' His response was cut short by a loud mechanical sound emitted by an apparatus worn by the third member of their ad hoc group. The older man smiled apologetically, touched something in his pocket and started talking.

'Yes, dear…no, dear…as you wish, dear, bye-bye.'

'What on earth is that?'

'That, young lady, is an ether-phone.'

'But it's not implanted.'

'Obviously not.'

'Don't you have any implants?' He was also curious.

'Wouldn't dream of them.'

'But then you can't "imagine" either,' he added.

'Yes, yes, of course I can imagine – but yes, I am limited in the globality of the experience when compared to you people.'

'But, but that's terrible, life must be so flat for you.' She was thinking of all the virtual shopping trips she had imagined as a teenager.

'Maybe yes, maybe no.' They were intrigued.

'You yourselves have just mentioned how much the police interrupted an experience more or less negative for you both.' Their silence was their response.

'And I could bet that you both spend much, much more time experiencing negative moments than positive ones.' They both reacted at once. That just wasn't so, not true at all...but before either gave themselves the expression of a verbal retort, something within them, their inner critic, gave this strange man credit for speaking the truth. There was a moment's pause, and within the small bubble created by the threesome, in spite of a cacophony of conversations and movements in the great cafeteria, they each experienced it as...silence.

'Do you think that there is something wrong with me? Something that my psy has missed?' She was starting to feel a little angry; it happened quickly, as always. Her current psy was Jackie's psy, and she had highly recommended him, saying how intuitive and sympathetic he was.

She had been seeing him now for some months, and had felt quite satisfied with the choice; he was at least as good as most of the other psys that she had seen.

But now, if it was true that she had some sort of problem that he had not noticed...She started to fade into the scene where she was once again telling Jackie off for her poor, inappropriate choices to do with the masculine of the species.....

'And so...?' He too was troubled, but maybe a little less so than her, he played absent mindedly with his beer glass. After all, heavy introspection was not one of his main occupations. The fine art of minute auto and hetero criticism was generally still the domain of the more contemplative sex.

'I just don't find the exercise of value,' the older man continued.

In spite of her flash of anger against Jackie, and the deep desire, if not to communicate it to her immediately, at least to experience communicating it to her immediately, she was drawn back towards the conversation in the present.

'It's like it's some kind of negative choice-point that I'm making,' she reflected, aloud. She was still feeling very uncomfortable.

'Well, you might consider it as negative, and if you accept that it is generally within your control, well, I'm afraid that I would have to agree,' he stopped and sipped a little of his tea.

'We're choosing to have negative experiences?' He spoke more in the general than the personal, then mirroring the gesture of the older man he sipped at his beer, the other smiled gently back at him, as if drinking in unison had a specific value.

'Actually, it's just a little worse than that,' he responded.

'Worse than that!' How much time and energy and credits had she spent on psys these last years? And here was someone telling her that it was even 'worse than that.'

'Yes, yes of course. You see, that by living most of your time either in the past, or in the future, you are by definition not spending time in the present.' The younger man seemed to be following the conversation better than she was, but that was largely due to the dozen or so other conversations that she kept starting in her head with friends, family and the afore mentioned, psy.

'And so what's so important about living in the present?' He was starting to lose interest in this conversation a little.

'Yes, what *is* so important about living in the moment?'

After all, she did spend almost half her life fantasising about what might go wrong in her life, and the other half discussing it with her girlfriends, or at least that was what Dave had shouted out at her as he left the apart for the last time. - Although she had hardly noticed, already talking of his awful behaviour on a party line to Alice and Jackie.

'Only', he looked up from his tea', that you could be missing a "good moment."' He spoke the last words as if they had a very special connotation.
'A good moment?'
'Yes, miss, a "good moment." Like, for instance, what are you drinking, sir?'
'A beer.'
'How is it.'
'Cold, quite good actually.'
'Take a moment. Concentrate on the taste, on the smooth refreshing feeling as it slides easily, effortlessly down your throat. Notice how the taste flows across your mouth and tongue, how you breathe in the flavour, and how that breath, slow and long, descends, descends into your lungs. And how on exhaling, you start to feel a gentle sensation of relaxation, naturally expanding through your body. And if you continue to concentrate, it seems that a small warm sun is shining out of you from your very centre, like a smile, the rays brighten and lighten your whole world.'

'And you,' he turned towards her, 'just stop worrying about how you are inhaling, and enjoy the moment, the "good moment."' And so she did. Yes, she continued to follow the flow of sweet air into her lungs, but from there onwards she allowed herself to be more and more lost in the pleasant, slightly heady sensation.
'Are you happy?' he suddenly demanded of them.

'Well....considering that I'm likely to lose my job next Monday…'

'…and I've just blown any chance of getting married this month…'

'Are you happy *now*, in *this* instant, here with your beer and maj?'

'Well, yes, I suppose so.'

'Well, I – I have an important appointment with some friends, that I'm going to be very late for.' The reaction to project herself into arriving late, with four hungry faces turned towards her, hungry for both food and gossip, began to grip her psyche, but she butterfly-brushed it aside. She stopped, toked on the n.a.c. (not a cigarette –ed.), closed her eyes, enjoying again the warm sensations as the cloud of pleasure breezed through her person. A warm, timid, childlike smile formed itself around her lips. 'Am I happy *now*, *this* very instant, *this* instant alone, *by itself*? Yes, yes, I suppose I am, at this moment, yes, you could say that I'm happy.'

'And so you're saying that we have to only live in the moment, never in the past or the future?' He was interested to ask.

'Not at all; there are happy memories in the past, and wonderful projects for the future.'

'So I mustn't think of anything negative that has or might happen?' She really should record this or write it down. Where did she leave her 'book'?

'But no. The errors of the past and the possible problems in the future are also important.'

'But those are negative.' He didn't like to think that someone was making fun of him.

'Not if they serve to help us analyse what we have done wrong or need to do right.

When you think of your past relationships, do you just get angry and upset, without succeeding to see what you can do differently? And you, is there anything that you can do now to change this man's attitude towards you at work now?' Their 'no' was silent but elegant.

'But I'm always thinking and worrying about the bad things that might happen, because. because they often do.' At last she had a point that this smug little man couldn't refuse.
'And isn't it normal to remember when someone had been totally unreasonable?' He saw a response about to form itself within the other man facing him. 'And if it was somewhere my fault, shouldn't I feel bad about that?' There: game, set and match.

'Maybe,' he smiled generously at them, 'just maybe the reason that you both are so attracted to continue thinking about these things is because, somewhere, within yourselves, you both know that there are things to learn from your experiences. And until you, "get the message," say, to speak, it keeps flashing up in front of your minds.'

The strange ringing tone starting again from his direction. At the same instant, the polite voice of a traffic police official could be heard in the heads of the two others.
'Good evening, this is police unit 40079 of the mid-western freeway. We are pleased to inform you that the white-way, transversal tunnel is now clear of the heavy traffic build up experienced this afternoon and has been re-opened. Safe route.'

The man put away his phone, stood up, smiled. 'My wife will give me hell if she thought I was "wasting my time" chatting like this. Good route.' The next moment, he had disappeared.

Then, they had….., a good moment…

1.2

David is sweating, but this is now more often due to the exercise regime that he has taken up. Today it is because he has just run up the stairs to my office, all four floors.

His grandmother has died, which saddens him, yet at the same time her death has helped release his fear of the future.

'Death is the only certainty,' he quotes, 'but if we don't live now, we are already dead.'

2.2

Hanna has found a boyfriend who is also a bit of a mongrel.

She has ceased to suffer anguish about who she is and where she came from. She now feels that 'I am just who I am,' for whatever that might mean.

3.2

I am taking a short break; I am sitting on an old metal swing. My three-year-old daughter, Kyra, comes up to me and asks me to take her on my knees and swing her on the swing. I put my work down and pick her up.

To and fro, to and fro, we swing back and forth.

I look into her beautiful, happy, smiling eyes.

I realise that I am happy, happy in the moment.

I continue to swing with my daughter; my doctorate and tomorrow can wait.

I am having a good moment.

Discussion:

There are many psychological and spiritual approaches that speak of living in the present moment and benefiting from it.

Like many of us, I had also often heard speak of the idea but it was only during a moment of inattention that I found myself, accidentally, doing it.

Since then it has become a discipline. It is not obvious, it is not easy, it is not even 'normal.'

What it is, is a way to enjoy life, the only moment that is real, is now. (Deep stuff, this!)

Remember, if you are lost in anger or worry or hurt due to a past or future event, you might just be missing a 'good moment.'

12: Transformation

1.1

Meg is a failure, and she looks it. She enters timidly into my office; badly cut hair, glasses, shapeless clothes, 19 years old and 'bad in her skin.'

She has been referred to me with the hope that, somehow, using hypnosis, I can do something to help against her chronic tension headaches.

Before starting to use hypnosis I almost always take one or sessions to investigate the patient's circumstances and history.

As a systemic-orientated psychotherapist I am acutely aware that a patient's symptoms might only be a signal of alarm and simply removing these symptoms might be negative, if not particularly dangerous. (You wouldn't suppress the warning light in your car that shows that your engine is overheating would you?)

Everything seems normal; her parents are both successful professionals, and Meg has a good relationship with both of them – in fact, she idolises her mother.

Somewhere an alarm bell starts to ring in my head – something doesn't feel quite right – I ask to see the mother.

Mrs Graham is magnificent, 57 years old and yet she looks no more than 37; confident, successful, beautiful. Nobody could compete with her!

2.1

Jack Mathus is angry, he is angry against everyone; angry against his wife, his children, his ex-employers, the medical profession but most of all,

Jack Mathus is angry against the cancer that is killing him.

There are no easy answers of how to deal with a situation like this one.

Jack is a good person, he has done no wrong, been a good son, a good husband, a good father, a good employee – but now at 53 years old, he is going to die!

I vaguely remember some of the 'steps of coping with impending death:' disbelief, anger, denial and eventually acceptance.

I confirm the prognosis with the hospital; between three and 18 months is the estimation; there are already several metastases starting to develop.

I call a family meeting. Everybody is tense. Of the three children, the oldest girl (24) has already left home, the son (20) is studying communications technology and the youngest daughter (18) is finishing her BAC, (high school diploma) .

Everyone swings between sadness, anger, despair, frustration and total hopelessness.

There is much work to be done.

3.1

I am walking on the 'front' (the boardwalk) of Blackpool, a sea-side holiday resort in the north of England.

My father has been forced to retire due to ill health (blinded by his diabetes), and he asked/pressured me into taking over the Laurel and Hardy exhibition that he had created.

The first year it had been quite successful, but this year I feel that all the visitors who might be interested have already visited it, and I'm not even covering my own wages.

I am also lonely, I cannot find anybody here that speaks my 'language' of personal growth and spirituality.

Transformation
From Tales of Peter The Pixie

It was a bright autumn morning and Peter the Pixie was just finishing his breakfast of grilled newts, brown toast and dandelion tea. Peter stood up, gathered together his breakfast dishes, from the smooth, plain pine table and, humming a little song to himself, went into the kitchen to wash up. Just as he was rinsing his knife and fork he heard a soft tap, tap, tap on his front door.

'Come in!' shouted Peter from the kitchen. The door opened, and in came a beautiful little fairy.

'Hello Elli,' said Peter emerging from the kitchen, 'is there something wrong?' For Elli was not her usual cheerful self.

'It's the Fire-Dragon, Peter. I think that there's something very wrong with him.'

'What do you mean?' asked Peter.

'Well,' said Elli, thinking hard to explain, 'he's, he's, he's not being very nice.' Now, to anyone that didn't know the Fire-Dragon, someone 'not being very nice' wouldn't be any cause for concern, but for the noble Fire-Dragon this was very strange behaviour indeed. Peter stood and thought for a while, and, as thinking wasn't what he did best, the strain was starting to show.

'I know,' he finally said, 'why don't we have a nice pot of tea, and you can tell me all about it?' And so they did.

Quite soon they were sitting in front of a gentle, little fire in Peter's simple, rustic sitting room.

It seemed that the Fire-Dragon was acting very odd, being rude and unhelpful and, as Elli had said, 'not being very nice at all.'

'I've an idea.' The tea had helped Peter to think clearly. 'We'll go and find Timothy, he'll know what to do.'

Timothy, the earthy, old toad, was happily sleeping in a pile of fallen leaves, the cool autumn sunshine was just the perfect temperature for the grizzly amphibian.

'Hello Timothy,' called Peter.

Timothy opened one eye.

'Mornin' Peter,' answered Timothy, closing the eye.

'Could you please help us, Timothy?'

'Oh, 'ello Elli,' said Timothy, finally rousing himself, 'what's the problem?'

And so they told him.

'Trouble is, no-one knows too much about fire dragons, them bein' from abroad, but let's go and see if we can do owt to 'elp.'

The first sign that there was something wrong was the discovery of a large notice, some ways off from the Fire-Dragon's cave. The notice read: 'Please to be informed that this is the private property of the Fire-Dragon, trespassers will be consumed, enter at your own risk, or better, not at all!'

'I can see what you mean about his not being very nice,' said Peter.

'Ello there, is there anyone in?' No answer. 'It's us.'

'Go away, you're not welcome here.'

'But it's your friends, Peter and Timothy and Elli. Please, Fire-Dragon, do invite us in.'

'Go away, you are trespassing, you have no right to be here.'

'Put kettle on anyway, because we're here now.'

'GO AWAY!'

'He does sound very angry. Hadn't we better do as he says? After all, this is his home, and I'd hate anyone to force their way into *my* house,' Peter reflected out-loud.

'Not unless they'd just baked a fresh pie,' replied Elli.

'And,' added Timothy, 'this part of the forest belongs to all of us. Just 'cus 'e's in a bad temper don't mean 'e can take over 'alf the forest.'

'And,' continued Peter, thinking that maybe he had sounded a bit cowardly and selfish, 'and because we are his friends, and maybe he needs some help.' And with that good thought, they entered the lair of the Fire-Dragon.

'Well, what do you want?'

'Hello Fire-Dragon, we've come to see you.' They had now arrived in the Fire-Dragon's rocky lair. It was particularly cold and dark. He had lit neither fire nor torch, and all his fine furniture was piled up in one corner.

'So, now you've seen me, good afternoon. And just what are you gawping at?' Peter was staring closely at the Fire-Dragon's body.

'What's happened to your beautiful scales?' For indeed the Dragon's honey-golden scales had lost all their lustre and had turned to a muddy brown colour, quite ugly and drab.

'I said good afternoon. Are you all deaf as well as stupid?'

'Now that is in'eresting. What do you think Elli? Some kind of flu maybe, or a form of tree bark infection?'

'It is very rude to ignore a person, and totally unforgivable to talk about them as if they don't exist.' The Fire-Dragon was getting very angry by now.

'I really don't know, Timothy. I can heal most things, but the legends of the Fire-Dragons are so old...' she sadly shook her head.

'Will you please pay me some attention.'

'We are paying you attention. Don't you 'ave any idea what's wrong with you?'

'There is nothing wrong with me that being left alone won't cure.'

'Do you really believe that?' asked Elli gently.

The Fire-Dragon became silent for quite a long while, then he wearily shook his beautiful head.

No, I don't.' And two huge tears welled up from his great golden eyes. The others didn't know quite what to say.

'But a cup of tea can't do any harm.' and in walked Peter with a tray, 'I couldn't think of anything to do that could help, so I made some tea.'

'Well that was a bloody good idea.'

'Thank you Timothy,' said Peter, feeling quite chuffed with himself, 'I thought rosehip might be nice for a change.'

And so it was. The Fire-Dragon lit the fire and some torches, while the others pulled out the table and some chairs. They all sat quietly for a while and drank the tea. The Fire-Dragon was the first to speak.

'I keep getting so irritable. Everyone seems to be picking on me. I am constantly having to keep extending my property to stop people trespassing on my own space.'

'Does that make any sense?' asked Peter, screwing up his face in an effort to understand the Fire-Dragon's logic.

'T' the Fire-Dragon it does, and that's good enough for now.'

'Oh,' said Peter, and settled down to enjoy his tea again.

'And now I have become so ugly nobody likes me anymore.' Elli stopped sipping her tea, and just looked at him over the rim of her teacup. The Fire-Dragon considered her silent reply.

'Well, maybe that part isn't totally accurate.'

'Who is it that doesn't like you anymore?' Again the Fire-Dragon considered the fairy's reply.

'*Me – I* don't like me anymore. I'm ugly and selfish and nasty and mean and I'm not even truthful anymore. These things are not acceptable in a Fire-Dragon.'

'So why don't you change them?'

'Easier said than done, Peter.' Suddenly Elli looked up.

'No, you're wrong, not for *you*, you are a Fire-Dragon. Fire-Dragons are *magical*, you can change yourself, yes, yes, in fact you must.'

'I'm sorry, I don't quite follow you.'

It had all suddenly become clear for her. 'We all live to a natural cycle, whatever we are; Pixies, Toads, Fairies, Butterflies, Snakes, even Dragons. Every so often the outer form that we have taken on becomes old and starts to die. The new inner us needs to take on a different, new shape; bigger, better, more beautiful. It's not people that are restricting you, suffocating, trespassing – it is your old shape, the old you.'

'I don't understand,' said Peter, scratching his head.

'I'll explain later. Go on Elli, you're doin' fine.'

'Fire-Dragon, now is the time of change, your old form is dying, if you don't let go, you will die with it.'

'How do I let go?'

'Give up everything that you have; your space, possessions, even yourself.'

'What will I then have?'

'The openness to receive what is to come; the freedom for the new you to form.'

'Will you, my friends, stay with me?'

'Of course we will!' they all chorused together. And with that, the Fire-Dragon set himself down on the floor, closed his eyes and…

HE RELEASED EVERYTHING.

The air became very still. They could each hear their own hearts beating. It became cooler and cooler, their breathing became quieter, it was very, very still. The cave darkened, they could hardly see each other, the Fire-Dragon was just a dark shape on the floor.

And then something very strange started to happen. They heard something drop, like a piece of hard slate onto the solid floor, and a narrow, bright, golden beam of light burst from his shape, another slate and another beam, then another, and another, and another. More and more, quicker and quicker the slates dropped and the beams broke forth from the body of the dragon, and the cave grew warmer and brighter, and the beams joined and melded and bathed the room in the most beautiful golden light.

And then, before them, resplendent in his brilliant coat of exquisite sunlight stood the Fire-Dragon.

'Happy Birthday, Fire-Dragon!'

1.2

Ms Margaret Graham confidently enters my office; her hair, now shoulder length, losely tied back, no glasses (contact lenses, I presume), quietly but elegantly dressed, 20 years old, 'well in her skin.' She has retaken her BAC ('A'-levels/high school graduation) in a private school and is now contemplating her options – and for some reason or other, no more headaches.

So, what has been the source of these miraculous changes? We hardly practiced any hypnosis or any long or complicated psychotherapy.

It was the mother, who decided (who knows exactly why?) to change her style and leave the space open for a new, beautiful, successful woman to represent the family.

2.2

Jack Mathus is dead, the remaining family members have requested one last session.

They enter quietly, yet all seem quite serene. 'We just wanted to share with you some of the last moments of Jack's life – it just seemed important and appropriate.'

They recount the holiday that they had all taken together in the South of France and talk of all the special and privileged moments that each one had spent with Jack these last months, but mostly how Jack had 'discovered' the maxim: 'Live every day like it might be your last' – and so he had.

3.2

I am officially unemployed. I live in a small caravan. I am an associate member of the Findhorn Community.

I am at peace.

Again, I am making some sense of my life.

Discussion:

This is a children's story but it is not for children. The things that we hold onto; inappropriate relationships, frustrating jobs, old self-images, unprocessed bereavement and the general obsolete clutter of our daily lives – these are adult concerns.

We fear the lack, the emptiness, the loneliness, the poverty that release brings.

Try this experiment: Cup your hands together and scoop up as many small pebbles or sand as you can. Next, being careful not to lose any, pick up a flower. – Get the point?

Happy   (Re) Birthday.!

13: The Pyramid Child

1.1
Donna is wearing a thin but baggy jumper. She has just been let out of hospital because she had dropped down to 61 lbs (28 kilos.)

She is my very first patient.

She explains to me that not only is her father very absent because of his work as a commercial traveller, but her mother invades all her space, even insisting that she knows better what Donna is feeling than Donna does. – Donna is 26 years old.

And of course the mother controls everything that she eats and does.

(This story was created for her.)

2.1
Benny is a good-looking young man; he has tight, black, curly hair, deep, brown eyes and a charismatic smile.

However, there is another side to Benny; he has a habit of losing his temper, quite often. And when he loses his temper, he screams, he breaks objects, he even cries with rage.

At 27 he still lives with his parents, which seems to be a good idea for everyone because, as he is still studying, his parents don't have to support him financially.

He, in turn still benefits from all the luxuries from living at home.

3.1

My father runs a travelling salesroom. We travel from town to town setting up a temporary department store in various locations, for several days at a time.

He offers my brother Lloyd and I the chance to undertake an independent run and to have a share in the profits.

We work very hard and are happy to calculate that we have earned a nice little profit.

On returning, our father re-calculates the figures, adding in many expenses that he had never mentioned when calculating the profitability of his own sales runs.

He informs us that we have, in fact, made a loss!

Disappointed, we never try to work independently again.

13 The Pyramid Child

The hot sun rose, fine mists of light sand danced in the morning breeze, still cold to the touch. The stately Nile filed past. The heavy pain of loss dragged her life energy towards the icy silence in which he now lay, waiting, waiting for death to release him, back to the warm world of the sun.

She felt the small movement from deep inside her body, again she was overwhelmed with sadness; he would never meet his child, his child would never meet him. All the riches that were hers to command could never bring him back, only time would.

The high priest sadly shook his head There was no question, she would lose the child, her last contact with the only real love of her life.
'Time will steal your child from you.'
'What does that mean?'
'Time will steal the child that is all that I can say.'

She sought counsel from all she could find, she must not lose this child, it must stay alive for her. She was ready to do anything. The old priest folded his greying robes over his aged body, there was little difference between the texture of his yellowing skin and that of papyrus scroll that he was reading with difficulty.

'You want to keep your child alive?'
'Yes, yes, more than anything else.'
'For how long?'
'As long as possible of course.'
'Forever?'

'Forever, you mean eternally alive?'
'Hmmm, hmmm.'
'It is possible?'
'It is possible.'
'Then she could meet up again with her father.'
'If she waited long enough, maybe."
'But what must we do?
''I will explain…'
The priest explained that the child would have to be housed in a specially constructed pyramid, designed to reduce the effect of time passing, due to its specific geometry. The pyramid was to have seven chambers, each enclosed within the others, each chamber blocking out more and more of the sun's radiation. So that, within the seventh chamber, there would be no effect of growth or change. The child would be fed a magical root from birth, which would allow it at some point to survive without food or water once within the pyramid. It would be kept isolated from all but its mother all its young life, and taught to be happy away from human contact. Maybe a small animal, say, a cat, could be introduced into her life as a permanent companion. She must enter the pyramid before fully entering adolescence or else it would be too late to arrest her continuing maturation…

And so the work on the pyramid began.

The baby born was a beautiful little girl, raven-black hair, deep, deep brown eyes. She was showered with all the luxuries that could be purchased; games, scrolls and for her third birthday she received the most wonderful, intelligent, playful cat.

Of course she saw no one but her mother, and she was instructed that on her tenth birthday she would be taken to a special room where she would live with her cat and await the return of her father.

As she had no other points of reference, all this she accepted, happily and contentedly, for that was the way that things had to be.

And so, on her tenth birthday, she was taken by her mother to the pyramid.

On entering through the first door she noticed a very large animal lying on the ground.
'Is it dead, mummy?'
'No child, it has been put to sleep. The animals are here to guard you. After the doors are closed and locked, if anyone should try to enter, they will wake up and attack the intruders.

And in each chamber there was another animal, only, as each chamber was smaller than the last, the animals were, in turn, smaller.

At last they reached the inner chamber and, as each door was smaller than its predecessor, by the time they came to that last door her mother could not enter. It was very beautifully decorated, with golden curtains and silken cushions. All her treasures were already there, but most of all, her wonderful cat. In the centre was an extraordinary crystal. From every side it emitted different colours of light, a fantastic prism, not only splitting and reflecting light, but somehow creating it as well. Finally, the daughter turned to her mother to say good-bye.

'Don't cry, mummy, for I shall be happy here, playing and waiting. Good-bye.'

She kissed her daughter, comforting herself that at least she would not die, as was prophesied, but would live alone but happily until she would again meet up with her father, whom she had learned to love, even in spite of never having met him. And she contented herself with this thought – that, and a small portrait that she had had drawn over these past few months. And so she departed, locking each door behind her as she left...

The girl listened attentively to the departure of the older woman; step, step, door, lock, step, step, door, lock...The sound faded further and further away. She looked around the beautiful room, full of everything she had ever treasured, and many more treasures beside, thoughtfully added to the selection.

'Come on,' she turned to the cat, 'let's go and play...'

And so the years passed...

Outside of the pyramid seven years had passed, but deep, deep, deep within the thick walls, time and change were excluded. Each day passed much the same way; waking up (somewhere about nine o'clock), attacking the cat, hugging, stroking, playing.

Morning prayers were the first activity on getting up. At ten, a half an hour for a bit of physical culture to keep the body healthy. Then more playing with the cat, to relax. From there she would go and pull out some toys, often families of dolls. She would play at how people would talk to each other, at work, at home, friends and families. Of course, families were an important source of inspiration.

At twelve she would turn the first hourglass. (There were two hourglasses, each one for exactly twenty-four hours, marked off for each hour. The first was to be turned precisely at twelve o'clock noon, the second at one o'clock. The reason for this double system was that, if for some reason or other she forgot to turn the first timer, she could resume the system with the second). Then mid-day prayers and meditation.

At one o'clock, after turning the second timer, she would have a little sleep for about an hour, and on waking up, more torturing of the cat.

Then at two o'clock it was time to study, to exercise the brain. She had already memorised the majority of the scrolls that were in her possession, so she would either re-examine the material from memory and discuss their contents with herself, or she would practice her reading.

And then, and only then, would she allow herself her favourite pastime, communicating with the cat, exercising of her higher functions.

Whether she was particularly gifted, or whether it was due to the special brew that both had had to drink for years, or whether it was simply the fact that they were together every moment of every day, but after a quite short time (time had so little meaning now), she found herself more and more able to 'talk' to the cat. The serious exercising of this function had now become a regular part of her daily routine. In truth, they were now so in tune that focusing time for this had become quite unnecessary, but she was a little obsessive in her habits, so she continued just the same.

Six o'clock was her time for singing and dancing. This would always finish with dancing with her cat, falling on top of her, and generally much laughing and joking.

Evening prayers would follow, to which she would often add some soft chanting, or very soft singing, for she had a wonderfully soft voice.

Then she would re-read, either in her head or written, some funny stories before finally returning with her faithful companion to her soft, soft bed.

But today, today something is different, there is a change, a new sound, a soft, rubbing sound.
She moved to the place of this new event, near one of the walls. There seemed to be a movement under the sand. What could it be? They watched and they waited. From somewhere deep, deep down there was something moving, something wanted to come up, come out. Something from underneath was surfacing into her life.

The something came nearer and nearer to the surface. Suddenly it was there; the something was a large rat. The cat let out a loud meow, arched its back, flattened itself along the floor, its tail lined up behind it and…
'No!' the girl shouted. The cat looked up. 'Leave it alone.'
'But why? It's for playing with, trapping, eating.'
'We don't eat.'
'But, but I want it.'
'I said no, and I mean no.'

The rat was looked on amazed, looking from one to the other.
'I must be going crazy', it said to itself.
'Why?'

'Because I can understand what you are saying, both of you. Oh my gods an' goddesses, now I'm talking to a cat and a human.'

'And?'

'It must be this pyramid, I've felt that it was strange from the first.'

'So why did you come in then?'

'I just felt this need to, but don't you worry, I'm not staying.'

'Please.' These were the first words that the cat had spoken for some moments.

'You don't need a rat to play with. Goodbye then, Mr Rat.'

'Just before I go, just tell me, what are you both doing imprisoned here? Have you committed some awful crime?'

'Oh, heavens, no,' she laughed, 'we have chosen to live in here.'

'You have chosen to live in a prison?'

'This isn't a prison, this is our home.'

'Okay, if this is your home, how do you go out?'

'We don't.'

'Could you?' Here, for the first time, she stopped.

'We are here to stay alive, and to wait for the return of her father,' the cat said.

'And when might that be?'

'It is not for us to know.'

'Is that right?' He turned towards the girl.

'Yes, that is how it is.'

'But if you wished to go outside…?'

'I think that I'm going to play with you for a while before I eat you,' interjected the cat.

'We don't want to go outside. It was our choice to come in here, and it is our choice to stay in here. And I forbid you to eat or play with the rat.'

'But don't you miss being outside?'

'There is nothing to miss, we have all that we need here.' The cat's tail began to agitate the fine dust on the floor.

'But there is everything outside.'

'We lack for nothing.' Her whiskers twitched. The preparations for launch were nearly completed.

'Nothing?! You live in a dingy old crypt – how can you lack for nothing?'

'Dingy old crypt? How dare you?! This room is the most beautiful room that ever existed. My mother has furnished it with the very, very best of the best.'

'Best of the best, it might have been, but now…' She had not noticed how the years had taken their toll on the furnishings; the carpets were nearly threadbare, the covers of the pillows were also worn, the beautiful curtains had lost their shine, even the beautiful crystal of light had dimmed through the years.

'My mother furnished this room with love and care. We love this room, we are happy here.'

The muscles throughout the cat's body, coiled. The rat sniffed at its feline adversary.

'Because something was right at one time, it doesn't mean that it is right for all eternity.'

'For us it is.' She sucked in the air. The rat glanced quickly at the young girl, who made no move to restrain the cat. Suddenly there was a small shower of dust, and a small hole witnessed where the rodent had been.

'Such a waste, such a waste,' pined the cat.

'It would have been wrong to hurt the rat,' the girl retorted.

'Such a waste.'

The next morning the cat rolled over sleepily and then stopped.

'What's that?' Her whiskers twitched.

'What?' yawned her still half asleep companion.

'That, that smell.' The cat jumped, reflexes suddenly operating again after years and years of inaction. She was all over the place even before her human companion could fully wake herself up.

The cat dashed here, there and everywhere, she stretched, yawned and look around her. Strewn across the floor were garlands and garlands of fresh jasmine flowers.

'Flowers!' She ran to them, laughing and crying. She buried her nose into the soft, sweet fragrance. She swam in them, she threw them into the air, she danced with them.

The cat did not join in her pleasure, but prowled around and around – if that rat would show even *one little whisker*, she would catch it, and that would be the end of it.

Needless to say, the girl did not play with the cat as usual. She also forgot her morning prayers. Nor did she bother to play with her old, worn out toys (as she now saw them.) She even missed turning the hourglass. And it was only because the cat woke up from a grumpy sleep in time that the second timer was turned when it needed to be.

'You see, you see. Even a little contact from the outside has disturbed our wonderful, worry-free life. If I see that rat again, it won't live to see daylight!'

'Oh, don't be so grumpy; it's a wonderful gift.'

That night, for the very first time, she dreamt of being outside, of lying in an oasis full of fragrant flowers.

The next morning she awoke quickly and sniffed the air. The sweet smell of the flowers continued to fill the chamber. She got up, eager to see if the rat had returned again. And so it had; figs, grapes and olives were scattered here and there.

'Oh!' she exclaimed. It was so long since she had tasted anything. They tasted so very strange and wonderful. Unfortunately, she wasn't able to swallow anything, as her body had temporarily forgotten how to take in food, but just the same, it was wonderful.

'Well?' She turned round in surprise. She hadn't noticed the rat entering, maybe it was there all along, watching her taste the banquet.

'Well, what?'

'Do you have everything that you might want in here?'

'Yes, we do, thank you very much. Even a new plaything.' The cat prepared herself to pounce.

'No, no you mustn't.'

'He's not going to escape this time.'

'You leave him alone, he's my guest.' That was of course the end of any chance for the cat to trap the rat. The codes of politeness he been read and discussed at great length by the two of them, and one didn't eat one's guests.

The rat waited patiently for the girl to reply to its question. She hesitated.

'We have everything that we want and need, thank you,' she purred.

'I can answer for myself.'

'Then tell your guest, that he can leave.' Something struck her, a random thought, a chance remark had set off a new train of thought.

'He? Are you a he?'

'Well, I've never had to prove it before, but if you would like to…?'

'That will not be necessary, thank you, yes it's a male.'
'Oh.'
'What's wrong? Have you never seen a male rat before?'
'I've never seen a male *anything* before.'
'But you do know what men are?'
'Of course I do. I've read all about them. I even have a likeness of my father so I can recognise him when he comes back for me.' She ran to a shelf and dug out the old, worn image of the handsome, middle-aged man.
'I can see why you should wish to wait for his return.' The cat, for the first time, seemed satisfied with one of the rat's responses – it didn't last for long. 'But I've never heard of anyone ever returning, and more than that, many of the older mummies have started to rot.'
'Blasphemy!'
'Truth!'
'A guest respects the customs and traditions of his hosts.'
'Customs and traditions, yes, but un-truths, no.'
'You think that my father may never return?' The words did not leave easily.
'Of course there's no way to know.'
'Of course he will. Haven't we read over and over again how the dead return? Isn't it one of the most basic truths of our society. Could it possibly be otherwise?'
'Could it possibly be otherwise?'
'Don't try your smart answers on us, inch-high.'
'But could it possibly be otherwise?'
'Can you possibly question your mother and all the sacrifices that she has made for you?' Added the cat.
'And just what has she sacrificed for her?'
'Everything, ten years of her life to keep her constant company, a massive part of her fortune to build this pyramid and her chance to be with her only child, to share in her future.

To see her grow, to see her marry, to see her have children, to never see her grandchildren.'

'That's some sacrifice.'

'My mother has sacrificed all for me.'

'So you see, it just could never be "otherwise."' The cat smiled sweetly at the rat.

'I see. Because you mother has sacrificed so much in this belief, then what she believes has got to be true.'

'Well, well, well, yes.' She seemed slightly troubled.

'What are you trying to say, rat?'

'I am only trying to understand the logic of your argument.'

'You're a male; you think differently – we, we have another, deeper, more meaningful way of ascertaining the truth.'

'Illogical.'

'Based on thoughts and feelings.'

'And your way of testing the truth is to look at how much has been invested in it?'

'What are you trying to say, Mr Rat?'

'Only that it seems impossible for you to question your beliefs simply because everyone has invested so much in them and to question them would mean that you might have all made a terrible mistake, which would be too awful to contemplate.'

'We cannot question our choices because we could not accept the consequences of having been mistaken?'

'Exactly.'

'But we haven't made a mistake Mistress, we are right, it is clear. And you, I suggest that you shorten your visit just a little. Maybe now would be a good time to leave.'

'No, wait. I want to talk to him a little more.'

'No, no, he only wants to make trouble, to upset our happy life, to destroy what we have waited so long for.'

'The rat stays; I command it!' And so he did, and they talked and they argued.

The cat (who had become quite learned during the years in the pyramid) quoted religious, historical, even legal texts to prove that their choice was correct. The rat listened attentively and somehow managed each time, to show how one might question each citation.

The girl sat and questioned, she questioned both of them. The cat became most unhappy that her mistress would think to question her position, because, after all, it was also up until now both the girl's and her mother's beliefs.

It was clear that slowly, inexorably, she was being won over by the rat's arguments...

'Maybe, maybe it wouldn't do so much harm just to go and take a look outside.'
'Do you realise what you are saying? To go outside before your father returns would destroy everything, everything that your mother has sacrificed to create. It would be a betrayal. Are you ready to betray both your mother and your father to pleasure a rat?!'
'You think that I really care? I was only trying to free you from your prison. I've lived in prisons, I've seen the souls of the prisoners shrinking, day after day, week after week. Nothing changes on the outside, but inside – inside it's horrible to watch. But you, you who have the means to leave, who keep yourselves imprisoned, living each day the same, frozen in time, it hurts to see. For me? No, not for me.' And in the twitch of a tail, before the dust could settle, he was gone.
'There, you've upset him.'
'I was *this* close to eating him, guest or not.'
'But couldn't he, just possibly, be right?'
'Not at all. We haven't yet made the morning prayers. Come on.'

It was the poetry that clinched it.

Some days later, on awakening, she noticed a small scroll, attached to small cord, hanging above her head.

In reality it was the cat that had awakened her. For the last few nights the cat had slept, as only cats can do, with its eyes half open. She was sure that the rat would return, and she wanted to make certain that no new surprises appeared. She had noticed the small scurrying sound entering the chamber and had even followed the movement on the inside of the silk curtain that covered the slanting ceilings and she saw when the scroll began to appear through the hole made by the rat. She waited patiently for the scroll to come out far enough for her to jump and grab it; unfortunately, the rat had other ideas. It was precisely because he expected the cat to try and thwart the girl receiving the item, that he had thought to suspend it from the cord attached to the curtain.

Of course this drove the cat absolutely crazy. First she waited for the paper to drop down, then, when she realised that it wouldn't descend further, she had tried to leap and grab it, but of course it was tied much, much, much too high for her to get to. It was finally her cries of rage and frustration that awoke the girl.

'What's the matter? Oh, oh I see! Let's have a look at it then.' She jumped up a little and easily caught the scroll.

'Don't look at it!'

'Why ever not?'

'Because he has brought it.'

'And?'

'He's trying to convince you to betray your parents.'

'That's not his point of view. And anyway, I don't see what could be so dangerous about a single scroll, there can be no argument that has to be written to have a value.'

She opened up the papyrus, slowly reading the script. The cat watched, irritated as she read and reread the contents.

'Well, what does it say that's so important?'

'I'll read it to you.'

'If you must.' The cat feigned indifference, badly. She recited:

'The sun rises over the Nile,
The boatmen rejoice,
The reeds sing,
The trees bow.
The girl fills her gourd with golden waters
To carry home
The morning's glory."

'Nice, isn't it?' asked the rat.

The cat reacted instantly to the rodent's presence.

'What do you want now?'

'Nice, isn't it?' The cat's remark valued no response.

'It's very beautiful.'

'I thought so, too, that's why I brought it to you.'

'And what benefit is there in bringing this poem to her?'

'Nice, isn't it?'

'Don't you see? Out there, there are beautiful things that we don't know of.'

'And therefore have no reason to miss. We are happy here, we have all that we need.' She repeated her little mantra.

'Nice, isn't it?' He repeated his.

'You're saying that I'm missing out, my living in here.'

'No, not at all – all that I'm saying is that I find that poem very nice.'

'It would be also *nice* to crunch your thick skull between my teeth!'

'Nice, isn't it?' And with that, he left.

It was difficult to define exactly at which moment she decided to leave the pyramid. It was more the way that a heavy see-saw or balance is weighed down on one side, the other attracts an increasing load which begins to weigh down more and more, the balance starts to shift, but the original burden and its own inertia resist the change, until, sooner or later, a critical mass is achieved and the movement is definitive.

She tried the little door; it was locked closed.
'There, you see, it's not even possible to leave of your own choice. You'll just have to wait until your father returns.' She did not even try to hide her satisfaction.
'Maybe I can manage to do something.' The rat climbed up the door and pushed his head and front paws into the little keyhole.
'If I could just…yes, I think that I might be able to…there!'
He flung himself out and into the air, a fluffy firework. 'I did it! I did it!' he screamed.
'If you pass through that door that will be the worst insult that you can imagine doing against your mother. I really, *really* don't think that it's a good idea.'
'I know, I appreciate your trying to stop me doing something that you are sure is a big silliness, but somewhere, even if it seems totally stupid, I feel deep, deep down that the rat is right.'
And with that she opened the door and began her journey back towards the outside world, to leave her safe refuge where time had no meaning, where each day was exactly the same as the last, a place devoid of change and growth.

They entered into the first inner pyramid. The space was very narrow, no more than two or three steps between the two sets of walls. She didn't notice the small step down and fell headlong onto the floor, only narrowly missing banging her head on the facing wall.

'Oh!' she cried out. It was then that she saw them; a small pair of beady eyes suddenly flashed open. She cried out, crawled onto all fours and scampered back into her room. The door banged shut, there she sat, her back propped up by and blocking the door, a door behind which laid danger and the unknown.

'Oh my gods, oh my gods,' she sobbed.

'You see, it's not for you to go out there.'

'Yes, yes you're right. Did you see it? What do you think that it was?'

'Don't even worry about what it was or might be, we're safe enough in here.'

'How strange, how very, very strange.'

'What's strange?' She looked up at the rat without moving her back from the door.

'I thought that they were all dead and stuffed.'

'What are you talking of?' She stopped crying.

'The animals – in each part of the pyramid there are animals. I thought that they were dead.'

'No, no, no, they aren't dead.' She vaguely remembered something that her mother had spoken of on entering the pyramid. She got up and started to walk; she was the type of person that remembered things better while walking. 'They are in a type of sleep and they can only wake up when someone enters, and then they will savagely attack the intruder. They are all vicious creatures, taken from all over the world.'

'Well, I must say, that's news to me.' They all turned as one to look to where the voice had come from. The door had not properly closed and when the girl had got up it had opened slightly. The little creature with the huge teeth was just pushing his way into the room. 'Savagely attacking people, vicious creatures? Please, please, please, that in no way fits in with my own self-image.'

The creature stopped, yawned gapingly, looked around at the assembly and said, 'Hello everybody!'

'So, you're not an especially dangerous beast?'

'My dear Mr Rat, are you trying to mock me, an honest beaver?'

'Actually, I was simply clarifying the situation for the ladies.'

'But my mother said…'

'Young lady, fortunately I have never met your mother and if I ever did, I would ask her to keep her negative opinions of my conduct to herself. I am a kind, loveable, woodland creature. Granted, I know how to defend myself and my territory, but gratuitous violence that is really not me.'

'You see, your mother is not always right about everything.'

'Don't you ever give up?' The cat's whiskers twitched and her tail began to beat the floor.

'Only when I'm wrong.' He turned away from the cat and back to the girl. 'Well?'

'I suppose that there is nothing to stop us trying to continue.' Her long-time companion gave an ugly stare, but remained silent.

The next lock was too big for the rat to open and there they would have remained stuck if the beaver hadn't had the good idea to gnaw a small opening in the bottom of the door.

She slipped down to the floor. Her eyes had already become strangely accustomed to the feeble stream of light flowing through the crack. It was then that she screamed. Although it might not have been so big, its two curved, spiked tusks driving towards her was more than enough to make her wish to have never opened any doors.

'Apples, apples, do you have any apples? I'm staving, starving.' The boar stopped and sniffed her. 'No, no, I can't smell any apples.' And with that he lost interest, turned and went back to lie down. Her body was still shaking when all the others had entered into the chamber.

'It could have killed you.'

'You've always something negative to say, haven't you?'

'It's by listening to you that she almost got killed.'

'She did not almost get killed.'

'But I was very, very scared. I can still feel my body shaking.'

'I think that we should go back before something really bad happens.'

'Yes, yes, I will go back. What, what's happened? The hole – it's got smaller, I can't get back through.'

'It's because you've got bigger.' He had scampered up the side of the wall, and was looking down at her in a puzzled way. 'Humans don't usually grow that quickly.'

'It's because you've left the chamber – quick, bite a bigger hole so that she can get back before it's too late.'

'Who elected you my boss?' The beaver was not used to being ordered about.

'There is no time to argue, just make the hole bigger – you can discuss our social positions afterwards.'

'But why do you want to go back? What has changed?'

'Why don't you just make the hole and stop chatting?'

'Because I don't want to. Do you wish to try and make me? I'm a little bigger than the rat.'

'Maybe,' the rat reflected from his safe position at the top of the wall, 'maybe it's exactly the sign that you shouldn't go back. The fact that you have already changed this much, means that what and who you were before has ceased to be forever and now the only road open to you is to go forward."

'That is a lie,' she spat out at the rodent, 'you know very well that the beaver could make the hole bigger and she could return.'

'But never as before. They are right, you know.' She had tears in her eyes. 'Yes, we could manage to back into our room but I'm different now. I couldn't stay, we've already gone too far.'

This was not the last time that this conversation repeated itself; each time that the group found itself blocked by a door – bigger, thicker, stronger than the last – the cat would re-open the discussion. As for how they finally managed to get through the doors, it quickly fell to the very animals brought in to block the passage from one chamber to the next to force them open. One also might note that as they advanced and the girl continued to change and to grow, the cat's discourse turned from arguing to simple complaints.

Hence they had succeeded to advance towards the live, changing world. There were only three doors left to pass through. The problem was that the animal guarding the chamber was a lion.

Although potentially very appropriate to frighten off persons attempting to invade the inner parts of the pyramid, as a means to break open the door it was totally under-powered. They sat, discussed, disputed, complained and criticised. Eventually the rat had an idea.

'I'll go and see what animal is in the next room.' It was a large, powerful horse, but the rat could not wake it up.

'It must need the presence of a human to bring it back to life,' he concluded.

'But she can't get in there to wake it up, you ridiculous rodent! I told you that this was the worst of follies,' said the cast, lazily, victoriously washing her face with a paw.

'Maybe she doesn't need to have her whole body in the room to wake it, maybe just a little part of her would do.' The beaver turned and started to gnaw at the door.

'What are you thinking?' she looked up, tears had streaked her now blotchy face.

'That maybe just a part of your body would be enough to awaken the horse.'

'I think you're wasting your time.' The boar got up in response, give the cat a nasty grunt and...

'Why not give it a try just the same?' And with that he began to pick at a spot on the door with one of its tusks near where the beaver was working. The rat disappeared through a crack in the door and began to nibble from the other side. The others all waited.

Finally the beaver backed away, saying, 'I think that it's nearly there, but I'm sorry, I need a little rest.'

'Well, I'm bored with waiting,' said the ram, who was not the most patient of animals. It turned its back to the door, lifted the hoof nearest to the work in progress and give an almighty kick. There was a scream from the other side of the wood.

'What's going on?!'

'Sorry, rat, didn't remember that you were there. I think it's time for a little direct force.'

The rat scampered out of the way just in time to escape the ram's flying hoof.

'Well?' Someone asked, "is it working?'

'I think that I felt something move a little.' He kicked again.

'Yes, it's giving.' And with a few quick kicks the wood started to splinter, and then it was open.

'What do I do now?'

'Just put your arm through as much as you can, maybe wave it about a bit.' And so the girl did.

'Hey!' She pulled her arm back through, and wiped the horse's saliva off of her hand.

'An outstretched hand with no food in it – what sort of business is that?' laughed the deep voice on the other side of the door.

'Could you please, please help me? I need for you to kick down this door.'

'Well, I suppose that I could do with some exercise, but isn't this door meant to be here and locked for a reason?'

'Yes, yes it is, you are quite right…' Whether it was the beaver or the boar or both that melted the cat into silence, is not important; that she ceased to speak was clear. The animals patiently explained to the horse the reason why they were all there and why it was important that they could leave. Eventually they all retired to the far end of the room as the horse put its hind legs into full activity. It took a very long time; the door was very, very thick and the horse had to stop several times to catch its breath. Finally the timbered block began to splinter and crack, and the congregation moved through to the penultimate chamber. By this time most of the blotches had cleared up but the girl was almost fainting from hunger. The cat was also looking a little grey.

'I'm sorry, my dears, but if this next door is any thicker than the last, I'll never break through it.' The horse looked quite miserable.

'Never mind,' said the beaver, 'there's sure to be an even bigger animal in the last room.'

'But even if there is and it succeeds to break open this door, it will also more than likely not be strong enough to break open the last door.'

The animals turned to attack the feline voice of negativity only to stop horrified. She had aged, her pure coat now heavily peppered with grey.

'What has happened, what has happened?' Again tears streaked down her cheeks.

'She is also ageing, as you are.' Suddenly the rat looked most sad. 'For this I am sorry. I hadn't realised that you would age so.'

'We must go back! I have to go back! I must, I must!'

'You cannot go back now; it is too late. I will return to the chamber. There I will retire into sleep and there I will wait. And when you go and return I will be there waiting for you. Good-bye."

They watched silently as the old, grey cat turned and left.

It took a long while to make a hole big enough for the girl to pass her hand through, but eventually it was done and the great sleeping beast was awakened. It listened carefully and quietly to their story and asked them to repeat it twice as he hadn't quite understood it all. At last it was understandable enough for him, so he walked to the far wall, pointed his massive horn towards the door and charged.

"Ow! That's a thick tree! Are you sure you can't find another way to open it?'

'There is no other way. Please, please try again.'

It took the beast three brave attempts before its strength gave out.

'It's no good, I'm not strong enough.'

'But it's starting to give way, I saw it start to break.'

'Are you sure?' The rat nodded back to the horse. 'Then maybe we can finish it off from this side.' And with that the horse gave a series of almighty kicks.

The door began to splinter and break. After that it was just a matter of time before the concerted efforts of the other animals succeeded in releasing themselves into the outer-most chamber.

'But now what? My little one is almost dead and I feel so bad and there is still the biggest door in front of us. What was it all for?'

She looked and felt totally exhausted. In a gesture of total misery, propelled by a totally illogical unconscious drive, she turned the great handle.

And the door opened.

The sunlight was intense; it made her feel even more sick and dizzy. She stumbled out of the magical pyramid, hardly noticing the great key that was sitting in the lock.

Leaning against the hard rock wall was an old woman. The pain of sadness had etched deep lines into the sun-baked hardness of her withered face. Folded into her arms was a faded likeness of a beautiful young girl.

How had she let time steal away her only child?

1.2

We have set up a system whereby Donna is trusted to control what she eats and moves into a halfway house.

Her goal is to start a professional school in another town in four months' time.

She reaches her target weight and starts the course on time.

Fours years later, she has finished the course without problem. Her weight remains stable, although she still has some food issues to resolve.

Now, all her food issues are resolved and she has a full professional, social and family life.

2.2

Benny has left home; it has been a very painful experience for all concerned.

However, Benny no longer has fits of temper or breaks things.

I reflect that maybe he doesn't have all that energy to spare after cooking, cleaning and tidying for himself.

3.2

My brother finds a similar job with an employer who appreciates him enormously – they become very good friends.

I leave to go to university in another city.

We both find our individual paths towards independence.

Discussion:

This is a story that is directed towards those who have a problem with maturing and separation from the parental environment. It speaks to both those that have the problem of leaving and those that have somehow difficulty letting them leave. This includes the eating disorder of anorexia.

It is a very, very long story; it is meant to be. Often the road to independence and liberty is very long and not at all obvious. The gift of a person being themselves, being free, unchained, unfettered is enormous but sometimes it needs fighting for.

The reasons why a young person might have difficulty growing up and leaving home, (in all the senses of the term, specifically including the emotional aspect), can be many and varied, but there are some 'classic' situations. The (eternal) youth has an important job keeping the parental couple stable; by creating a focus for their attention or by supporting a weaker partner. The other theme is that of 'waiting' *as a child* for a relationship with one or both parents, where an important part of the child/parent relationship has been missed.

If you are maybe the 'child' in this story – 'give up on your parents!' It is not for you to save them or to wait for them – go, grow and live your life.

If you have a child that is not growing as it should, stop worrying about him/her and look to what you can do to improve your own life.

14: The Flower

1.1

David is about forty, forty-five years old, quite short, with slightly greying, well combed short hair. His suit is a little tired looking, a little rumpled, a little shiny on the elbows and the back of the legs. He walks with some difficulty, he stoops, he looks much older than his years.

David has a chronic lower back problem; he takes painkillers daily, sleeping pills at night and he has regular physiotherapy sessions twice a month.

The therapies do help, but he still suffers considerably. X-rays have not revealed any problem that can explain his discomfort, other than the lower vertebrae, which are a little too close, as though slightly compressed together.

His family doctor has noticed how David is very often tense, and although constant pain could be one explanation, he has suggested that maybe some sessions of relaxation might also be of help ...

2.1

Ann and Steven are a young couple; they have been together for just a few months. However, things are not at all as they would like.

Last year Ann broke up from a long-term relationship when she found out that her partner was cheating on her.

Now she is having great difficulty opening up sexually and emotionally.

No amount of re-assuring from Steven of how much he loves her or how he has never been unfaithful has had any effect.

He even organised a meeting with his ex-girlfriend so that she could witness that she had never had any reason to question his fidelity.

Although Ann acknowledges that she has no good reason not to trust Steven, she still is not succeeding to open up to him...

3.1

Mona is twenty-eight weeks pregnant with our first child. She is confined to bed-rest, due to crises of contractions.

She is often in great pain, but, worse than that, she is scared for the health and safety of our baby.

Yet another series of contractions start. She tenses up, the pain and fear mount.

I run a warm bath, she tries to relax a little...

The Flower

Pain and tension, whether physical, emotional or psychological form a perfect, vicious circle.

Whichever comes first, if it succeeds to activate the second, unless and until this mutually re-enforcing system is interrupted, pain and tension will continue to worsen.

However, to try and block, or force to re-open, or to relax, will only activate the same mechanism which will resist and thence re-enforce the tension and pain.

Patience and gentle coaxing are needed to calm the little, scared animal in self-inflicted pain into trusting enough to release its grip and to let itself fall into the protective, comforting arms that await it.

For this exercise allow your hand(s) to close into a quite tight fist. If you also have a pain that might be linked to tension, allow your mind to also notice this.

This applies equally to emotional or intellectual tensions.

During this induction your hand can open more and more, following the course of the opening of the flower.

You might very likely feel releasing of the other tensions during and after this induction.

The Flower

The night is cold and dark;
The moon is high;
The stars dance.
All is calm,
Serene,
Asleep.
The flower sleeps,
Its head bent low,
Its petals tightly folded.

The dark becomes less clear,
The cold more intense.
The moon descends
And stars begin to fade.
The world holds its breath.
Tension.
The flower shivers
With fear,
The head even lower,
Petals even more closed

The sky whispers of light;
The moon falls;
The stars become vague memories.
The cold bites;
The day waits to enter.
The tension increases.
The flower shivers
With anticipation.
It rests totally immobile;
Head and petals.

Bands of radiance cross the horizon;
The sun promises.
Clouds exist.
The day begins,
The cold blunts,
The tension relaxes,
The flower shivers
Into awakening;
The head senses the dream of change,
The petals stiffen

The blue pales,
Washed by the light of sun.
The day has awakened.
The air excites,
The cold fades,
The flower responds;
Its body enters into movement,
Lifting the head,
The petals sense the change.

The sun floats gently into day,
Cushioned by a quiet haze.
The air exults the birth.
The temperature is warming.
The flower responds;
The stem directs the
Raising head in the direction
Of the light;
First response.

The sun passes the horizon,
The day has begun,
The air loses its last chill,
The birds break into gentle song;
The head straightens,
The very tips of the petals
Unclench.
The sun mounts,
The insects stir,
A quiet blue invades the sky.
The stem is sure;
The first layer of petals
Begin to separate from the head –
Gently, little by little,
The silken arms
Extend.

The day has fully arrived;
The sun has settled.
On its skyward course
A warm breeze
Floats
Gently
Across.
The flower,
Breathes
The first prayer.

Little by little,
Inch by inch,
The petals
Release their tension,
Relaxing,

One after another
Opening,
Softening;

The next layer,
Already prepared,
Actively,
Impatiently,
Awaiting each its turn.
Ready,
Release,
Relax…
And again,
    And again,
            And again.
Ready,
  Ready,
    Ready.

Release,
      Release,
        Release.

        Relax,
    Relax,
Relax.

The day advances;
Birds fly;
The sun imposes his
Presence.
The flower
Dances,
Loosening her veils;
The last layers of petals
Open,
Revealing
Inner secrets

The day hangs heavily;
The sun is in his power.
He reigns down
His golden manna.
The flower responds,
Absorbing,
Enriching,
Opening her deepest,
Richest self.
And so –
There she is;
Open,
Vulnerable,
Pure,
Relaxed.
For so is the state
In which
She can profit
The most
From all
That life
Has to offer.

1.2

David exhales deeply; he is slumped on his chair, a little like a puppet with no-one holding the strings. Another deep expiration and he starts to straighten himself up; he stretches and tests his back by moving it tentatively side to side.

He is waiting for the aggressive, painful sting that usually accompanies the movement…it doesn't come. He gets up carefully, smiles, nods and leaves.

The pain will return; we are both aware of that, but the short-term relief is much appreciated.

It takes six months before he succeeds in letting go of all he needs to let go. Fortunately, that also includes his bad back.

2.2

For Ann and Steven it is, strangely enough, Steven that responds most to the experience.

He explains in a later session how he imagines himself giving out warmth and comfort and of how Ann will open, little by little, to his energy.

Ann is happy, too; she feels 'unthreatened' by Steven, and that is helping her to relax and open to him.

3.2

My wife arrives at term, she is in a light trance.

The midwives question whether she is really in labour, as she shows no signs of pain or discomfort.

Our daughter is now twelve years old.

Discussion:

Tension begets pain and fear and sickness and suffering.

It also closes us from our free flowing energies.

Relax and release these tensions;

Trust life that if you open to it,

It will feed and nourish you.

Set free the suffering,

Liberate pleasure,

Inhale life;

And exist

Fully.

15: The Baker

1.1

Sue comes to see me. She seems a very normal, middle-aged woman, a little overweight, appropriately dressed and made up. She works, she has three teenage children and she has managed to successfully juggle work and family.

However she is now starting to lose it and she is in constant conflict with her husband – often over money issues. He is mean; he has always been a little mean, but now as the children are getting older the problem seems to be worsening.

I ask to see him but she informs me that it would be impossible; he could never put himself into question. Just the same, I insist that she ask him.

The next session, surprisingly, he has accepted to come.

I listen to his complaints that his wife and children are spendthrifts.

I ask him his story:

'I come from quite a modest background, where my father taught me the 'value of money.' My father encouraged me to save my meagre wages from my apprentice to buy my first motorbike. He was as proud as I was. I very much appreciate the way that I was brought up and I have always admired my father for it.'

I remark that it seems to me that for him 'one can never save too much.'

'But of course,' he responds...

2.1

It is a cool autumn afternoon. A hulk of man enters.

Paulo is generous, very generous. Friends can phone him day or night if they have a need and Paulo will be there. With his big pickup truck, muscular arms, mechanical and technical abilities, he is really the saviour in any moment of difficulty.

However, Paulo is not feeling his usual self, he is often feeling tired and irritable, his GP has checked him over and has found nothing physical, so he has referred him to me.

Paulo is an immigrant ex-alcoholic who has never known his father.

Last week someone rang up from another town, a 'friend-of-a-friend,' who had heard that Paulo might service his car for him as a favour as he didn't have much money.

My diagnosis of Paulo's problem is that of dependency/co-dependency – he is looking for the parental (father's) approval that was absent during his early years.

It is already dark, it is mid-winter, there is no snow but it is very cold.

Paulo is complaining to me that he has lost most of his friends and that it is all my fault.

He has set limits, as I have strongly suggested, as to how much he gives without receiving in return.

Many of his friends have not accepted the change, which they see as negative and selfish.

3.1

I am living in Canoga Park, Los Angeles; I am looking after the house of a friend of my father's, who also happens, for the moment, to be my boss.

It is quite a big house; television with cable, a pool table, musical instruments to play with, my own typewriter, a full-size swimming pool, a Jacuzzi, a big yank car (of course) and enough money in my pocket to get by on.

And of course, being alone, I soon start to feel lonely and depressed.

The Baker

Once there was a baker whose family had been poor, so poor that at times there wasn't even enough to eat, hardly even a crust of bread. The people around did not make any great effort to help this poor family. They said that the family did little to help itself, that the father drank and that the mother was a wretched, little thing who laid around the house all day, doing nothing at all.

It was true that the young man noticed that there was a difference in how his parents were, that his father was hardly ever home, and when he was, his mood could be very good or bad. He was also aware that his mother seemed to be interested in very little, even dressing, washing or cooking the little that they had to eat failed to motivate here.

As soon as he was old enough, he began an apprenticeship as baker, swearing to himself, that when he would have a family they would never want for anything, and that he would give nothing to anyone who wasn't part of his own family.

And as the years passed the baker kept good his promises. He learnt well his trade, and after his parents, both of them old and infirm from hardship, passed away, he left his native village and opened his own bakery in a town quite some miles away. He married a woman of the region, and truly they wanted for nothing; they were wealthy, happy and healthy (although maybe somewhat stout.)

He was liked and respected by the some of the townsfolk, but his position of giving nothing to anyone that wasn't part of his own family went down badly with others.

Whenever criticised by others, he would remind himself what it was like not to have enough, to feel that emptiness inside, that deep, deep hunger. In fact, if he let himself, he could still feel that very specific lack – so deeply, deeply was it a part of his life experience.

Sometimes it might provoke a need to confirm that he could eat all that he wished, and so he would close up shop, take a large tray, walk round all the shelves, select any and every item that would catch his fancy, take it all down stairs into the bakery (located in his cellar) and very, very carefully eat the lot. Truly, he often had difficulty with the last few pastries, but somewhere he knew exactly just how much he could manage to eat, and that's exactly how much would be loaded onto the tray.

And so it came to be that one sunny afternoon the baker, having completed his work for the day, had left his wife to look after the shop and had taken himself off for a walk. He was crossing the main square when his attention was attracted towards the old, municipal fountain. He didn't know why, but he looked just the same.

There was a bundle of clothes, heaped up against the low wall; it moved, his heart jumped, 'Oh my God!' – No, it couldn't be, but yes, but no. He stood looking at his father, old, worn out, there he was…but no. No, no it wasn't his father.

On looking closer it was clear that it wasn't the same man, but the resemblance was still very strong and marked.

His attention towards the old man had provoked a reciprocal interest. The baker began to advance towards the old tramp. It was then that the warning light switched on: 'Don't give to anyone that isn't family!' He moved to turn away, but it was too late, the tramp was already walking towards him, a strange look in his eyes, a sort of recognition.

'Young man, pray tell me who you are, and do you come from these parts, or other?' Even the voice and the way of talking reminded him of his father. Taken by the spell of confusion, the baker let fall his defences and almost mechanically responded at length to the other's questions.

As it turned out, the resemblance to his father was not at all a coincidence; the man was in fact the youngest brother of the baker's father. The reason why they had never met was that he was raised in an orphanage after the untimely death of their father and he had never known any other member of his own family.

Of course the baker was touched by the old man's story and, even though he never gave to the poor, he kept his word of giving to his own family and offered to take his uncle into his home.
'You are most kind, but I am by nature an independent soul, I could not live on your charity.'
'At least come tonight and dine with us.'
'That would be most generous. At what time?'

The relative, although clearly poor, had had a disciplined upbringing and had served for many years in the country's army, so his manners were good, and he was appropriate and appreciative of the hospitality offered by the baker.

He was also full of many interesting and amusing tales.

As for his present state, he explained that as a young man he had passed some of his army years in India and was very taken with the old men who, at the end of their lives, give away all their worldly goods, and take to wondering the country, living off the charity of others. He had promised himself, there and then, to experience this style of living, trusting in the generosity of the world that he would always have enough to fill his stomach to survive.

They talked and ate and drank well into the night, and when finally the old man insisted that he leave, the baker piled him high with the bread and cakes that he had not sold that day. At first the uncle had flatly refused, but the baker pressured him, saying that it would only be good for the pigs the next day, so off he went, arms fully charged.

The next morning, after having completed his morning's baking, the baker climbed up into the shop to fill the shelves with the fresh, sweet breads and cakes still warm from the oven. He glanced out of the window to see a scruffy young man waiting, it seemed, for the shop to open.

This was one of the town 'lay-abouts,' always begging – someone that the baker had no time for at all.

'What do you want?' The youth was surprised as the door was flung open with some force, but the look of shock and surprise was quickly replaced by one of appreciation.

'Oh, it's you. Good morning, Mr Baker. I just came round to say thank you for the bread – you make really good bread. It's the first time that I've tasted your bread. Excellent. Thanks.'

And with that he strolled off. The baker scratched his head and went back to filling his shelves.

Some hours later a young widow came to the shop. She had a small baby in her arms and she handed the baker a note, smiled shyly and left. The note said, 'Dear Mr Baker, your generosity has filled my heart, as your bread has filled my stomach. Sincerely yours.'

It was his wife who, on returning from the market, was to supply the explanation for these strange events. It seemed that the Baker's uncle had seen fit to distribute the old bread and cakes given to him the evening before to some of the town's poorer inhabitants. She informed her husband that she had also invited him again that night to dine with them.

The night passed as the preceding one, with the Baker feeling impressed with the worldliness and nobility of his older relative. Again on leaving he piled high his uncle's arms with old bread and cakes, only this time his uncle received the food gladly and warmly thanked his nephew for his generosity.

After his uncle had left, the baker took to thinking; he had a problem; he had always sworn that he would never give charity to others apart from his own family, but now, through the agency of his father's brother, he was supplying food for the town's poor. What was also true was that this act, indirect as it was, made him feel warm and less hollow somewhere inside.

And so the days passed, the baker resolved his problem by not thinking of it – he was giving food to his relative, and what that relative chose to do with it was his concern, and not that of the baker.

What the baker chose also not to notice was that he had begun to bake a little more bread than usual, and that there was no demand for it. At the end of the day this extra quantity found its way into the sack that his uncle had started to bring with him each evening.

As the days passed the baker begin to produce more and more bread for the sack, leaving less and less for the baker and his wife, but if she mentioned anything, which she did from time to time, the baker called her heartless and mean, so she just waited and watched in silence.

They began to eat less and less. No more did he have his little binges; he no longer felt any need to prove that he could eat what he wanted, he was already feeling full of something positive.

Another effect of the baker's increased investment in the sack was that the baking of more and more bread meant that he had to get up earlier and earlier each day, as clearly he couldn't afford to employ any help.

One could say that the baker began to slim down, but it was more like he was melting away. At first everyone complemented him on this change, as he had allowed himself to become quite fat. The compliments pleased him and he began to take more and more interest in his appearance. No more would he finish his baking and, still half covered in a frosting of light flour, would he bring the produce into the shop. Now, after having finished his baking, he would take half an hour for himself, to wash and change into fresh clothes before entering into contact with the outside world.

At first his wife was pleased with the changes in her husband. He was more attractive, more positive and more active than she had ever seen him, but after a short while she became concerned. Was he working himself too hard? Was he losing weight too quickly? Why had he cut down his eating so much? Wasn't his mood becoming a little less stable? His responses were clear and logical, if not a little aggressive and defensive. No, he wasn't working himself too hard. In fact he was feeling that he had more and more energy. Of course he was not losing weight too quickly – it was just the natural process linked with his new found well-being. No, he had not cut down his eating too much; he was eating as much as he needed. And finally, he had never felt happier or more contented. If his wife was feeling something negative in their relationship, maybe it was because she was being a little jealous of his health and happiness!

It was some weeks later that the flu appeared in the village. Some people thought that it was brought by the gypsies who had briefly passed by the south road, others thought that it was carried by an ice-cold north wind that appeared and disappeared like an evil breath, but it was more than likely carried by a peasant that had come to sell or buy at the weekly market.

At first the Baker seemed particularly resilient, but as the days passed one could almost see the battle that the virus was having with his immune system. It was also about this time when the baker's wife began to notice that the stocks of flour and other basics were starting to run low but were not being replenished.

It was nine o'clock in the morning. She heard the shop door being knocked on, shook and knocked on again before all returned to silence. 'What was happening? The shop should already be open.' She went to investigate. The shop was empty, but she could smell the baking from the cellar. She opened the trap door, and climbed down to investigate. Her husband was curled up on the bakery floor, at first she thought that he must have had an attack or something, but on closer inspection she heard the speeded up, shallow breathing of someone quite ill.

She called on a neighbour for help and surprisingly easily they managed to lift him up out of the cellar and carry him up to his bed. The doctor diagnosed pneumonia, prescribed the necessary medicines and warned the frightened woman that her husband must not return to work for a long time.

What to do? What to do? She felt herself very alone in her predicament when suddenly she had an idea. Thrusting her bonnet onto her head, she ran out of the shop door. She found the uncle near the big fountain in the market place smoking his pipe and talking to a few down-and-outs. She quickly explained the situation to him. Strangely enough, his first reaction was a little half smile.

'One could see it coming, but don't you worry. I will see to the necessary. Please, may I have a set of keys for the bakery and the shop?'
She ran home, took out her husband's keys and hurried back to the old man.
'Now you go home and look after yourself and your husband. I'll see to the rest.'

The next morning the woman rose as usual, but that was strange. Other than Sundays she always awoke to the smell of fresh baking, and this morning – it was the same. She quickly dressed herself and ran down to the bakery to investigate. The bakery was full of activity. There were two men busily baking the day's requirements. It was difficult to make out exactly who the two were, but she was sure that they were amongst the town's non-working denizens. As she was trying to place the two faces more clearly, she heard the door of the shop being unlocked and opened. She went up to investigate. It was the widow with her baby.

'I'm sorry, but the shop is not open yet.' The wife was confused.
'It is now,' the widow smiled back, putting the baby and its carry-cot down behind the counter. She then shouted down into the bakery, 'Okay, Jack, you can start to bring the stuff up now!'

It took a moment to sink in that the widow was here to look after the shop, but when it did, the baker's wife started to panic.
'But no, no, I'm sorry, it's impossible, you can't stay.'
'But whatever is the matter?'
She broke down in tears. 'I'm dreadfully sorry, but I have no money with which to pay you.'
'Pay me? Pay me?,' she started to smile and then to laugh, 'but I've already been. For weeks now your husband's fine breads and wonderful cakes have changed my life from barely having enough to having plenty. Oh, and before you say anything else, the same goes for the two villains downstairs.

As for the flour and the rest, that's more down to the common folk in the village who have been touched to see your husband's generosity and have wanted to contribute towards it.'

The wife was very touched by the widow's words…
'Unfortunately, it seems that husband is a man rather of extremes. At one time he starved himself of sharing but then he changed and couldn't stop himself – a glutton for giving.'
'Yes, but I think that he felt so good when giving, it sort of filled him up with something that he needed.'
'But it didn't last.'
'No, he had to keep having more and more and more. And giving more and more and more, but he has always been a bit like that.'
'Maybe it's time for that to change.'

And so it did.

The baker recovered his strength and his health. At first he was still against eating much, but after a while he realised that the feelings that he had felt through not eating had been some sort of a mania, and this mania had made him feel irritable towards, even threatened by, others. As for the energy, it was a bit false; he could keep going for many hours over all, but during that time he would often have to take short breaks, and somewhere underneath he was always tired and, worse than that, he had become physically very weak and he would often have to make two journeys to carry what he could usually have done in one.

With the help of his uncle he managed to find a balance in which he could afford to employ the others part-time, give a reasonable amount to the poor (the scriptures talk of ten per cent) and still have enough for a comfortable life.

He inquired about the other baker, and learnt that he was an able man who had the misfortune to prefer gambling to baking, and of course had lost everything.

Now, having cleared his mind of the need to risk all he had for the thrill and excitement of the turn of a card, he had nothing with which to rebuild his life.

It was some weeks later and the baker was filling an order for a small party, taking his tray and choosing a variety of small cakes and pastries, when it struck him.

When was the last time that he had done that for himself?

When was the last time when he had felt that strange, hollow, empty feeling gnawing at his stomach? Of course the answer didn't matter.

The baker smiled to himself, took one of the little cakes and savoured every single bite.

1.2

I see the family for one last time.

The father has not really changed his attitude; it seems that he cannot.

What we have succeeded to do, however, is to thrash out a rough budget of how much he puts on the side to save and how much to 'spend.'

The next challenge, according to Sue, is to get *him* to buy *himself* something that he doesn't totally need.

2.2

It is spring. It has stopped raining and the sun is shyly peeping out from behind a cloud.

Paulo is thanking me; he now sees that the friends that he has lost were not friends at all, merely people abusing him.

Also, being more open to asking for and receiving help creates a good feeling – being loved and appreciated.

However, there are still quite a few unresolved issues, still much work to do.

3.2

I go into a piano bar and start to talk to the young pianist, I tell him about the musical theatre piece that I am writing. Might he be interested in collaborating?

A friendship starts up.

Now I am happy, but it's the *relationship* that brings value, not the material comforts.

Discussion:

A feeling of lack is an uncomfortable experience, but a deep, permanent all-absorbing emptiness is awful. This void, which notifies us of its presence as either a dull perpetual ache or the sudden imploding of an enormous black hole, can really gash the pleasure of one's life.

Whatever might be the root of this woe; poverty, loss, abandonment, coldness or other, - greed and meanness are not the answer. You can never take in or hold onto enough to fill that incredible emptiness – give it up!

The other way to try and cope is to give, give, and give (a more 'Christian' approach This can certainly give the illusion of well-being, but if it is too unbalanced, or is motivated by the need or an expectation that people will 'repay' your generosity, that cannot succeed either.

There is a natural balance of giving, a level that feels good, a type of giving that feels appropriate and for which no return is expected or looked for. When you give, exactly that much which feels good to you to give, where the pleasure rests in the act of sharing, if the other appreciates the gesture – then that is enough. When you give like that, then you are automatically filled with your own feelings of pleasure.

If someone gives to you, then you can fill yourself with the pleasure of knowing that in your receiving of their offering, you are allowing them the pleasure of giving to you

This is not total insanity.

16: Still Crazy After All These Years

1.1

Betty suffers from manic-depression. Over the last ten years she has been in and out of hospital five or six times. Although on a rather heavy cocktail of drugs; anti-depressants, mood-stabilisers etc., she now seems almost chronically depressed.

We work for almost twelve months, using a lot of hypnosis, on lifting her out of her depression and keeping her from re-descending.
The work bears fruit and her mood stabilises – until...
'Mr Gedall, I'm going into another depression.'

2.1

Valerie is an attractive 25-year-old; long, curly, brown hair, tall, elegant, well spoken, well educated. When I asked her, during the first phone contact, what her motive for consulting me was, she answered, a little vaguely – 'relationship stuff.'
Now she is here, in my office, and I pose the same question.
'Mr Gedall, I think that I might be going crazy.' I encourage her to continue.
'I believe that I can connect to other people's feelings and I attract people that are unwell or unhappy. They talk to me for a while, then they leave feeling better, leaving me feeling like shit.'
I ask her to imagine what it's like doing my job.
'Yes,' she smiles for a moment, 'but I can also feel what is wrong with them, like having cancer – it has happened several times. I really fear that I might be going mad.'

3.1

I have been in Switzerland for nearly three months now and things are not going well.

My control of the French language is minimal and doesn't seem to be advancing much, so I'm not comfortable going out to meet people.

As I have no right to work in Switzerland, I borrow some French francs from my girlfriend, take the ferry to Evian, France, and pass by all the temporary work agencies in the region. Even the odd one that accepts to put me on their books cannot find anything for me. Each time I borrow money for this fruitless exercise I feel worse and worse.

Mona is out all day; she has her year of practical work experience, she is working full-time out of town.

My mood is going further and further down – am I falling into a depression?

Still Crazy After All These Years

It is weird how even the most familiar places can look strange and different in the dark and in the rain. As the taxi turned into the road, Harry felt an odd feeling of uncertainty; was he actually in the right place? Nonsense, of course he was – look, there's the tree where the cat got stuck up and had to be rescued by the firemen. And there Dave Bingley used to live before his father went broke and they had to go and live above the fruit shop that they'd bought with his grandmother's 'shoe money.' Yes, of course this was the right place, it was only the rain and the dark, and maybe because he was sitting in the back of the taxi. For years now he had always driven himself home, if he hadn't walked, that is.

The taxi stopped as he had directed it to, just before the little track that used to pass into the open fields behind the house, long since overgrown with modern maisonettes. He paid the fare, and slid out into the cold, wet night. How long was it since he'd taken out this particular key, a round-headed Yale, with a very worn piece of red ribbon attached to it? To be honest, the ribbon now more resembled a dirty brown string, but it was a pretty red ribbon when his mother had first given him his very first key. 'Red ribbon for good luck.'

Holding his carry-all in one hand, he began to manoeuvre the key into its lock with the other, all the while wishing that he had thought to close his coat before leaving the taxi.
All of a sudden the door opened by itself, or so it seemed, and a strange woman's face appeared from behind it.

Being dark, both outside the house and in, he could make out very little of the woman's appearance. 'Well?' He was a little lost for a response.

'Can I come in?' She looked at him quizzically. 'It's very cold and wet out here,' he added as a kind of explanation.

'Who are you?' The question was asked in a very simple, matter-of-fact fashion.

'I'm Harry. I live here.'

'Oh really?' There was a little surprise in her voice. 'Maybe you'd better come and explain yourself.' Harry hauled his bag inside.

'Just put it here,' she directed him, 'and you come on in here.' She switched on the light in the living room as she ushered him in. He left his bag in the narrow hallway; a hallway that he knew well, also the equally narrow staircase directly in front; the first door on the right was the front room, the 'best' room that nobody ever really used. Once, before a priest had come to visit, he remembered his mother cleaning it from top to bottom. The second door on the right was the living room. It was here that this unknown woman was directing him.

'Harry, is it?' He couldn't quite sense what she meant; was it really a question, or a simple statement? He looked around the room. It was pretty much as he had always known it. The fireplace on the right wall, the same broken tiles, the same pictures of his grandparents, now both long passed away. At the back, the window with the table in front; towards the left, the step down into the narrow, long kitchen, where he remembered his grandmother cooking smelly meat to feed her old Boxer dog.

Out of the window would be the back yard, a small paved area, that had seemed much bigger when he himself was not as big as he was now.

She followed him into the room. 'So, Harry, is it?' He still couldn't make out what was behind that half-smile – irony, maybe. 'Are you better now?'

He caught his breath. Again he could feel his throat being gripped by the unseen assailant, the feelings of confusion, the knot in his stomach. Much, much less strong now, but just the same, the panic and anxiety were still there. He hadn't much liked the clinic; yes, they were kind and helpful, and after all that, he now felt well enough to return home.

Home, his home, the home of his parents, and, before them, the home of his grandparents. But who was this strange woman here now, looking at him is this particular way?

'Yes, yes, thank you, much better now.' He was starting to sweat, just a little, but he could feel the discomfort returning just the same.

'That's good, very good,' suddenly she smiled at him, 'but you've been away such a long time.'

'Not that long. It's only been a couple of weeks.'

'A couple of weeks – is that all you think that it has been?'

The world stopped, his thinking stopped, he stopped breathing. He felt nauseous, dizzy, he put his hand out to steady himself. It found the table, old, but still solid. What did she mean by 'is that all that you think it has been?'

'I'm sorry, I'm not following you.'

'Take slow, deep breaths. Concentrate on your contact with ground. The fear is not real. Take a reality check. Nothing is threatening you. Relax'. He tried one exercise after another. He didn't speak for maybe five minutes. And she, she just waited, watching him, gently smiling. Eventually, he pulled himself together somewhat and straightened himself up.

'Feeling better now?' she asked in a solicitous voice.

'Yes, a little, thanks,' he started for the kitchen.

'Where are you going?' she asked a little sharply.

'To the kitchen, to get a drink of water.' He did so. The familiar action relieved a little of his discomfort. 'Where are my parents?' he asked, returning with the glass.

She stopped for a moment. Took a little breath. 'I think that you'd better sit down.' He chose his father's chair, the one to the left of the fireplace, where one could almost see into the street if the doors were all open. It felt the same as it always had. He even had the same slight uneasiness which he'd had since childhood that his father would come in and chase him off his chair.

'You have been away a very long time.'

'But it's only been a couple of weeks,' he protested.

'Have you ever heard tell of your aunt Agatha?'

'Yes,' he felt confused again, 'yes, she had some sort of breakdown, but I don't know any of the details.'

'Your aunt Agatha has lived in an insane asylum for many years now. She had a complete breakdown, which is to say that she went completely crazy. For years she lived in a total delirium. When she finally started to recover, she had no memory whatsoever of what had happened during all the years, that she had been so ill.'

'And?' The panic was starting to return. He was falling, falling. He held on tightly to the chair, but it didn't help, he just felt that the chair was falling with him, spinning crazily, out of all control.

What was she trying to tell him? He knew of course.

She was telling him as gently as she could, her voice soft and caring, so gentle, supportive, even.

'How long has it been?'
'Years,' she responded, flatly.
'And my parents?' Breathing was so very difficult, so very difficult. He was drowning, there was nothing to hold onto, sinking sands, the world was a whirlpool and he was in the process of being sucked under.

He knew exactly what she was about to say; they were dead, and had been dead for years, and he had been in some crazy state. Maybe it was even their deaths that had pushed him over the edge. He closed his eyes, anything to block out the awful reality that he had no choice but to accept.

'Okay,' had said to himself, taking in a deep, deep breath, as he had been taught, 'it's now or never'. He opened his eyes.

'Oh, my God.' He was totally convinced that he could see his mother standing in the doorway in her nightgown. He stopped breathing once again. He was deeply in shock, he was hallucinating wildly, he would have to return to the clinic, he wasn't well enough prepared for the shocks he was encountering.

They shouldn't have let him out without telling him everything first. The 'ghost' looked first at him, smiled, and then turned to the woman. The woman smiled back at her.

'Put the kettle on, Agatha. Harry looks like he's seen a ghost, I think that he could do with a nice hot cup of tea…'

1.2

We discuss the situation and we find several negative events that have happened in the last weeks; an unexpected tax bill, the cancellation of a long awaited visit and a bad cold with a painful sore throat.

I reassure her that any normal person is likely to feel depressed with all these negative events happening at much the same time.

The idea that she might be 'normally depressed' seemed impossible to her, but she accepted my reassurances and promised to go back to her usual routine of support groups and regular gym sessions.

By the next week she was back to her usual self and the possibility of being 'normally depressed' has been re-enforced in her vision of her personal universe.

2.2

Valerie is feeling better with herself.

She has accepted the idea that people that have 'strange' experiences and are very aware that these experiences are *not normal*, are very rarely crazy. She recognises;

That there are many beliefs and cultures where these types of experiences are considered normal, if a little special;

That not being a 'dustbin' for the un-wellness and unhappiness of others is totally reasonable, and that there are techniques for protecting oneself from this;

That being appropriate in relationships means that one often accepts the negativity of the other, although each member is still responsible for what they bring into the relationship, and that if it is too strong, some temporary distance might also be a good idea

Putting all this into place is still going to take some time – we are working through it…

3.2

Mona has seen a poster – 'You said that you like to act. Would you like to be an extra in a play? It would at least get you out of the flat from time to time.'

I present myself, and even though I have little idea of much that is being said or is going on, I am accepted and participate, playing several small roles.

She then finds a list of short-term work experience places linked to psychology – I find one that I like and that accepts me; a small miracle.

I then find several 'student' jobs to fill up the rest of my free time.

I have no time to feel depressed and I notice that the negative feelings were purely circumstantial.

Discussion:

This is a story created with the intention of helping those that have experienced mental illness, anguish, panic, depression, etc., to begin to question their fear that any feeling that is similar to their illness means that they are back in the same nightmare.
Anguish leads to anguish, panic to panic, depression to depression.

There are two messages in this story:

First, and most important, that it is *normal* at certain moments to feel bad. Everybody, for instance, can occasionally feel a little low, even depressed, tired, lacking in desire, energy, a sense of fun. That is really okay; what is not okay is to worry that your world is going to end (again) and that two, three, four months of purgatory are at the bottom of the slippery slope that you are on.
Stop this 'self-fulfilling prophecy.'

The second message, which is just as important, is that there are life events and people, outside of yourself and your control, that are not your problem. Accept them for what they are, just as you can accept yourself for who you are – and get on with life!

17: The Petit Pause

1.1

Dr Jack Bowers is a junior doctor, which means that he has several years of working crazy hours ahead of him, as well as the responsibility of having people's lives in his hands.

Dr Jack Bowers is clearly not making it. He is tense, has random aches and pains all over his body, is sleeping badly and is, not surprisingly, chronically tired.

Of course his personal relationships are suffering, but, almost paradoxically, he must keep up a positive image in front of his colleagues. Thus, a medical certificate for a few weeks of rest and recuperation is totally out of the question.

- Do I have a magic cure, please?

2.1

Carole is a housewife with three small children, two big dogs and one very hard working husband – Carole has her hands full.

She feels that she is running non-stop from morning until night.

She is starting to lose it.

Last week she shouted at the children and kicked one of the dogs. She is now petrified that if things don't change soon, next time it could be the other way round.

We discuss how she might create some time/space for herself...

3.1

 I have taken over the running of a toy department in a small store. I am not at all satisfied with the way that the department is put together, however the store is open seven days a week and for the moment

I am working completely alone.

I work normally until 6:00 p.m. when the store closes its doors and I set to work re-organising the department.

Things are going reasonably well until I arrive at the 3:00 a.m. energy dip. I am painfully aware that at 9:00 a.m. the store will re-open and I will be obliged to have my department ready and functional.

But I cannot go on; I have worked all day and half of the night. I am exhausted. I need to stop.

The Petit Pause

This is an induction in three parts.

Place yourself in such a way – standing or sitting – that you feel comfortable and that your feet are well flat, in contact with the ground, with or without shoes and/or socks.

The first step is to notice the moment between the end of the expiration (breathing out) and the beginning of the inspiration (breathing in.) This is the moment of the 'petit pause'.

The second step is to allow all that is negativity to flow down, out of your body, through your feet, back into the earth.

The third part is to draw up all that the earth can give to you, all that you need and can use.

The Petit Pause

After the induction '**Le Petite Pause**'
created by Dr G. Salem

Find yourself a comfortable position, standing or sitting,
Feet flat on the ground; good contact.
Allow yourself to become more and more in touch with yourself,
Your thoughts, your feelings and, most of all, your body.
And central to your body; your breath.
How does your body breathe?
Notice its rhythm, notice its depth.
Inhalation; breathing in.
Exhalation; breathing out.
How it can become slower, deeper,
All by itself, naturally
Notice the air descending, descending,
Deeper, deeper,

And out, slowly out, out,
Until the moment
When all is out
And like
A swing or pendulum
On reaching the very top of its trajectory.

Stops.

Stop, pause.

And then…

Descends.

The air
Naturally
Re-descends.

The body
Relaxes,
Breathes
And…

Pause…

Allow
Your attention
To focus on both
The breath
And the pause

Take your time.

And Pause…

And Pause…

And Pause…

Now that you are beginning to
Relax
More and more,

It is the moment to notice your
Feet,
Solid, safe, sure,
Well in contact with the ground,
Being grounded, earthed, attuned, connected,

Opening channels for communication.
Maybe this favouring of flowing could bring unusual
sensations.

Your feet might feel bigger, wider, heavier,
Maybe stuck or melting, joining with the ground

Or maybe,
Just maybe,
You might imagine that, like the base of a beautiful, strong tree,
You are integrated into the mother earth;
The earth that absorbs, heals and purifies;
That earth that nourishes, feeds, refreshes;
A tree with roots, toes, that reach deeply, deeply down,
Down into that rich, black, warm, humid safety,
As you feel…

And now it is time to
Allow
Your body,
Your emotions
And your mind
To release
All that that they no longer need;
All the old stories, experiences, tensions, pains, frustrations,
All can now leave

How you might imagine this process is personal to you and to the moment.

You might just feel a vibration, a light tingling electric current, a warmth
Beginning at the very top of your head, gently flowing down, down,
Behind your eyes,
Down the neck,
Across the shoulders,
The length of the back,
The thighs, knees, calves
And into and out of the feet.

Or a liquid stream, flowing naturally along its own downward course,
Allowing gravity to draw all that needs to drain out, to run out, to seep out, to be out.

Or light or colour or energy... as you will.
All ways and means and presentations;
All good and right and useful;
All your own expression;
All moving gently or quickly onward and downward,

Filling the good earth with new sources of life
Which she will use and transform
To serve herself and all others.

Allow yourself to be emptied of all that needs to be emptied,
All that is heavy, old, sad, sick, weak, useless for you at this time,
All to return deep down into the very source of life.
Every single, last drop.

And when…
And when…
It is done
And all that has needed to leave, for this time
Has left, gone, departed,
Now, now,
Allow
The wonderful, deep contact
With the very source of
Richest nourishment
To begin to supply
All that one might want, need and desire in this moment;

All that is needed to
Cope with everything you need face, to
Combat all that needs to be fought, to
Conquer all that needs to be overcome, to
Cheer all that needs to be more joyful, to
Create all that needs to be born or transformed and to
Cherish all that needs to be valued, appreciated and loved.

And, as before,
Create for yourself
The image; experience the sensation
Of how and when this
Force of nature
Will flow
Up your body,
Filling every single molecule and cell
Of your innermost being
With the richest most wonderful
Energies,
Linking into and re-energising your own
Inner resources.

Notice how, from the very edges of your toes,
This flood of positive matter
Begins its journey of abundance
Refilling,
     Regenerating,
         Restoring,
             Revitalising...
Up, up, up
The calves,
Up to the knees,
Maybe a light or small vibration,
Slowly, steadily, or
As fast as you like,
The powerful thighs
Respond;
Level of the hips,
To the lower back

The breath can also participate,
Drawing in, drawing up
The life-force of the air, and of the earth;
Each cycle of breath brings in new energy.

The solar plexus.
The sun bestows its bounty,
A wave of warmth and light
Ripples over the land.
The plants grow,
Fruit ripens,
Flowers bloom,
The tree is strong and upright.

The heart
Fills;
Love,
Self and selfless,
Flows richly through each artery and vein

The lungs
Expand,
Bringing in
New possibilities.
The air calms or excites;
It too is a fuel,

And up, up, up,
Filling
More and more and more;
The dynamic vortex
Spirals into complex activity:
Neck, face and head

All is complete.

Take a deep breath...

Hold...

Hold...

Hold...

GO!

1.2

Dr Jack Bowers is doing better; much better, thank you. He is sleeping better (he has now also accepted to taking a sleeping pill from time to time), but his saviour is clearly his induction into the world of auto-hypnosis.

He uses auto-hypnosis to relax during pauses at work, to help him sleep and at various random moments of the day and night.

However, I feel that there might be another discipline that would serve him even more: meditation.

I feel that this thirst for the experiences found in auto-hypnosis, which I see as a short- to medium-term practice, is likely to respond well to meditation, which is a much more long-term solution for relaxing, rebalancing and re-resourcing.

2.2

Carole is doing better; she has enrolled her two youngest children in a nursery (the oldest is already attending primary school.)

After completing all her regular 'chores' she now manages to offer herself two hours per day to relax in one way or another, even to just sit and watch television.

3.2

I lie on the floor, even though I am cold and the floor is hard. It is such a pleasure to let myself stop and to close my eyes, if only for a little while…

I know that I cannot really let myself sleep; there is still so much to do.

I relax, I allow the tension to flow away, it empties itself.

At some time positive energy will arrive to take its place.

I do not think these thoughts, it is not a conscious process – I just feel it as the thing to do.

It is now 4:30 a.m. and I drag myself off of the floor. I feel groggy. I stretch and re-start work.

The tiredness has passed; I am again functional.

At 8:30 a.m. I tidy away most of the boxes and at 9:00 people can come in. I haven't totally finished – it takes another two or three hours of work until I am satisfied.

I slept well that night!

Discussion:

This induction is an exercise that is very easy to learn and to do.

It is relaxing, refreshing, energising.

It works for any situation or difficulty.

You can imagine using it to release tension, stress, anger, sadness, pain…

You can call forth strength, force, tenacity, creativity, humour, intelligence, patience…

It can be worked through quickly; a minute can be quite sufficient.

Or it can be slowly savoured.

Go on – try it; you might like it.

Part 2: A theoretical framework

1. A general introduction to some theories and terms used within the practice of hypnosis.

This work is written using ideas and concepts taken from clinical hypnosis sessions, which follow a style and philosophy created by Milton H. Erickson, 1901-1980, hence the term Ericksonian hypnosis. The other major current is that of 'auto-hypnosis', which will also be discussed below.

1.1   Ericksonian Hypnosis

Two principals are at the base of Ericksonian hypnosis, which differentiate it from other types of hypnosis. The first principal is the idea that a person's unconscious contains not only negative elements (desires and traumatisms, created and stocked by the process of repression, as in the psychoanalytic vision of the unconscious), but as also a 'reservoir of resources that could help a subject to help himself'. 'Ericksonian hypnotherapists emphasize the resourcefulness within clients and their inherent capacities for productive change' (Edgette and Sasson, 1995.)

Leading on from this first principal is a second that speaks of a 'non-directive' or permissive approach (as opposed to other hypnotic approaches which are much more directive.)
'Another significant departure was his conception of the hypnotherapist as permissive rather than authoritarian.' (O'Hanlon, 1987, quoted in Edgette and Sasson, 1995.)

Through this particular method, one supports the subject in contacting, within himself, the specific resources that he seems to lack, with the aim that through this contact the problem can then be resolved (or resolve itself).

In practical terms, what this means is that for the majority of the time, the hypnotherapist will suggest to the subject that he 'might wish to do something', or that he 'might feel something,' always leaving the person the total possibility to not follow the hypnotherapist's lead, and to end up somewhere quite different.

Another of Milton Erickson's favourite therapeutic techniques was to tell his patients stories.

'The "teaching tales" are stories that Erickson told to his patients and students over the years.' [Editor's notes] (Rosen, 1982.)

Before moving on to discuss auto-hypnosis, and later on how these tools and techniques can be used for self-help and personal development, it might be useful to define certain basic terms.

1.1.1 What exactly is hypnosis?

Dr. Gérard Salem (Salem, 2006) emphasizes that the term hypnosis refers to three types of phenomena: **the hypnotic state or the trance**, **the technique** used by the hypnotist, (one might note that leading someone into or inducing a trance state is generally referred to as **an 'induction'**), and **the type of interaction** between the hypnotist and his subject.

1.1.2 The trance

The trance is considered as a 'modified state of consciousness', which links the characteristics of a waking state (as confirmed by an EEG) with a specific type of experience of muscle-release/relaxation and dream-type productions. It is the experience of being *here* and being *there* at the same time. It is a totally natural state which we experience, in principal, about once every ninety minutes; this is a moment of distraction, a pause in our mental processing, when we lose track for a few seconds.

It's as if the mind stops 'to take a breath'. It is also a state that we enter while doing a boring or repetitive task; ironing, washing up, driving, even listening to someone droning on and on and on; some school teachers are excellent hypnotists.

What is so fascinating about this state is that we can be totally involved with an experience, with all our senses and yet *at the same time* be fully aware of our surroundings and be able to react instantaneously. Just think of the situation of driving in a car and daydreaming when someone cuts in unexpectedly; the reaction is pretty much immediate.

Another way to form an image of the trance is to liken it to the feelings just between sleeping and wakefulness; early in the morning when, for instance, one knows that the alarm has rung, that it is time to get up, but one allows just another five minutes to finish that nice, warm dream.

1.1.3 The suggestion

The suggestion is a key communicational tool in hypnosis, which allows the hypnotherapist to gently lead the subject where he judges it necessary for the subject to go.

(NB: As stated above, the subject is never forced to enter into or to continue an experience that he clearly does not wish to.)

1.1.4 The induction

The induction of the trance is accomplished through two methods:

The first is the use of a constant, monotonous sensorial stimulus (for instance a mark on the wall, the contact of the subject's hand on the material of his clothes or the 'classic' follow-my-watch – not currently used anymore), on which one asks the subject to focus his attention.

This concentration on a specific stimulus reduces, little by little, the awareness of the existence of other stimuli, and the monotonous nature of this particular stimulus provokes a phenomenon of sensorial adaptation which leads the subject to become less and less conscious of it.

Hence, through this process, the attention of the subject turns from the external world to focus more and more towards his inner experiences.

The second method is the use of a particular type of communication.

For example, one of the principal tools for the induction and the deepening of the trance is that of the 'body-subject language'. This is based on a type of verbal formulation within which one refers directly to a specific part of the subject as if it was an independent entity in itself; one might say, for example, 'maybe your eyes feel that they wish to close' or 'notice how your breathing has become slower and deeper.'

I also often make reference to the subject's body, emotions and mind as if they were independent but linked bodies/entities, with each having their own memories, needs, defences, logic and resources, which, although quite weird as an idea, in practice, proves to have a reality!

The resulting effect is called 'dissociation,' (being conscious of the outside reality, all the while experiencing a personal, other reality), and it is an essential characteristic of the hypnotic state.

Generally one of the first inductions that is offered to a subject is the 'safe place.'

This is useful for almost every case, and is also often used for subjects learning to use auto-hypnosis.

The 'safe place' is not necessarily a place at all, but a positive experience remembered or created by the subject, where they can feel good, relaxed, safe. Many hypnotherapists begin every hypnotherapy session with a return to the safe place, just so the subject has a psychic safety net to return to if they get into difficulty during the session.

The safe place is also a good experience that the subject can 'anchor' with a physical gesture, so that by repeating that gesture (touching themselves in a specific way, like folding their arms, placing their hands together etc.), they can re-centre themselves in a good feeling when faced with an external or internal difficulty.

1.2   Auto-Hypnosis

1.2.1   Introduction

As its name indicates, this method is a type of hypnosis that a subject practices on himself. The subject is taught and (often) coached on entering the trance state through the use of specific inductions. The manner of teaching auto-hypnosis might start by an experience of ordinary hypnosis or not, and the uses and benefits of a practice of auto-hypnosis are many and varied, as are the types of populations that use it.

1.2.2 The similarities and differences between
hypnosis and auto-hypnosis

The *only* fundamental difference between a hypnotist-led session and an auto-hypnotic session is that of the (vocal) presence of the hypnotist; other than that, the two processes are identical. This is to say that, for us, the principals and process are identical for an auto-hypnotic trance as for hypnotist-led hypnosis; in the use of a focus of attention on a monotonous stimulus for the induction of the trance state and for the patient to experience the sensation of dissociation, as his focus of attention is redirected from the outer world towards a deeper and deeper contact with himself.

However, each session of auto-hypnosis will follow, more or less, a predetermined path even though the patient might have learned a number of different inductions which they might use for different situations; such as general relaxation, against stress, for pain relief and / or to aid in getting to sleep.
A 'live' session with a hypnotherapist, on the other hand, can lead to any number of experiences and sensations depending on the wants, needs and desires of the patient at the time.

1.2.3 The differences between auto-hypnosis,
relaxation and meditation

One often asked question is, 'what are the differences between auto-hypnosis, relaxation and meditation?' If one looks at physiological reactions of subjects when in a trance state, deep relaxation or deep meditation, one finds a great deal of similarity.

Hence, if there is such a cross-over within the techniques, where is the specificity of auto hypnosis in which one finds the particular benefit in its use?

To begin with, auto-hypnosis, as with its 'big brother' hypnosis, is not a simple, single technique used for a unique purpose. It is a very general technique with many forms of entry and with a multitude of uses that can be adapted to a large number of situations or settings.

Generally, both relaxation and meditation are taught as specific trainings, with a single means of entry directed towards a single described goal which often needs a very specific setting. (Although one should not forget that there are many, many different forms and styles of relaxation and meditation.)

What I have found in my clinical work is: first, only a very small number of subjects are open, willing, capable and disciplined enough to undertake a practice of meditation and second, that relaxation techniques are only successful for a limited number of people and that it is very difficult to transpose the benefits of relaxation in a quiet space to an outside (or otherwise) stressful environment.

On the other hand, auto hypnosis is generally very well accepted by most subjects and the large choice of induction techniques allows for the subject to tailor the technique towards the particular circumstance and their own mood/personality/preference, and after a certain amount of practice an unconscious reflex becomes installed which comes into play in any situation where necessary.

(Of course one needs to nuance this statement with the reality that this still needs a real investment on the part of the subject and that this is only part of a larger therapy, and the automatic reflexes also have their own limitations).

2 The 'A, B, C, D' of Attitudes, Behaviours, Coping Strategies and Defensive Roles

Four methods of dealing with our daily lives

2.1   A Normal Process of Development:

The conscious, or what we call the mind, is a wonderful thing, linked with the unconscious and the semi-autonomous working of the body and the emotions; we are capable of learning about things, learning how to do things, how to act, etc, etc.

However, it is not the mind but mostly the unconscious learning processes that teach as how to react, to feel, to relate and to behave in the many and various life situations to which we are confronted.

Based on watching and experiencing the adults around us and getting verbal or non-verbal messages (as for instance smiles and open faces, or frowns and sighs); messages of positive or negative re-enforcement for certain reactions, attitudes and behaviours we learn how to be, how to cope and even in extreme cases, how to survive.

We all have needed to learn to cope with the many and various experiences with which life confronts us; babies, young children, even young adults have to deal with some rather difficult moments. These include the first experiences of frustration, of abandonment, of some level of violence (direct, indirect, intentional, unintentional, physical, emotional or intellectual), coping with anger, fear, pain, (of all types), shame, guilt, worry and anxiety.

These are the normal hurdles that every human being has to overcome.

Alison E. Parker and collaborators in a paper for North Carolina State University (Parket et al., 2002), quote L. Repetti (Repetti, et al., 1999): 'Major life stressors are known for their negative impact; however, minor daily stressors also disrupt children's lives,' and that, 'Experiences in middle school, such as making new friends, changing classrooms, and peer harassment, may increase children's exposure to stress.' By middle childhood, children have already developed a repertoire of coping strategies (Causey & Dubow, 1993.)

Here we see how quite early on, even within 'normal' life experiences, children have to deal with quite a large number of stresses and have to have in place strategies to face them. However, some of these strategies might not always be the best choice.

In their article on coping, Ellen Skinner and colleagues (Skinner et al., 2003), wrote: 'In the broadest sense, ways of coping … capture the ways people actually respond to stress', which again puts the concept of coping clearly into the range of normal, healthy responses to everyday life. Yet, they also add the precision that 'how people deal with stress can reduce or amplify the effects of adverse life events and conditions', which can and does mean that some coping strategies that we use have negative outcome effects.

Mark Dombeck and Jolyn Wells-Moran put it slightly differently (Dombeck and Wells-Moran, 2008): 'Apart from personality traits, people also tend to develop habitual modes and methods of managing stress and coping with upsetting emotions.

By and large, these habitual methods do help people to manage and defuse stressful situations they find themselves in, but they are not all equally efficient at this task. Some work better than others. While some really do succeed in helping people to manage upsetting emotion, the lesser quality methods generally end up causing more problems than they solve.'

The fact that we are capable of worsening our situations through inappropriate and inadequate coping strategies is not something that we are always open to see and to hear, but, then again, we have never consciously chosen the ways that we deal with life. As we have seen, ways of dealing with life are put into place from early age. 'The "taking on a role" is an unconscious act – it is not deliberate. These roles are played right through adulthood: they are part of our learning process. They are products of our environment (family, community & cultural)' (Tuinman, 2008.)

2.2   A Less Than Normal Process of Development

Yet over and above these 'normal' life challenges, depending on many internal and external life events, the challenge of coping with life can increasingly become a fight for survival.

When faced with situations of poor health (physical, emotional or mental) of a child or important significant persons, separations due to deaths, divorce or relocation, medium to extreme violence, (of any type), important financial stress or 'just' growing up in a less than fully functional family, the attitudes, behaviours, coping strategies and defensive roles that need to be stimulated are likely to be equally as extreme.

The two main groups that we often hear of are 'Survivors' (women –and some men– who have been sexually abused as children) and 'ACoAs' (Adult Child of an Alcoholic.)

One can see from a clinical point of view that the outcomes are very different. Survivors can often have clear psychiatric or psychological symptoms; Post-Traumatic Stress Disorder, Borderline behaviours, depression, eating disorders, self mutilation, etc. ACoAs can express their problems in taking on certain behaviours or roles that become exaggerated and rigid (see below.)

The likely reason for these differences is that sexual abuse often happens 'later' in the child's development and although it is an abuse hidden from the outside, the child is mostly aware that an abuse is happening to her, whereas a dysfunctional family has more than likely been dysfunctional since the individual's early childhood; the child does not necessarily feel directly personally abused (it happens to some degree to 'everybody') and by virtue of its social nature the child has the possibility to create 'social coping strategies'.

Klaas Tuinman (Tuinman , 2008), in his work with ACoAs, lists nineteen 'roles' that children can take on. He explains that these are '… normal reactions to severe dysfunction (especially from alcohol) - that become dysfunctional also (this means, they begin to interfere with leading a functional, successful and satisfying life.')

2.3   Dysfunctional Adults

At what point does the experience of childhood become so negative that we become dysfunctional as adults?

The answer is, of course, impossible to find.

However, there are many that suggest that we have all passed through critical, negative moments in our development and that we are all damaged to some degree or other; an extreme position perhaps, but one that can be well defended.

Maybe to stay with the concept that 'nobody's perfect' is reasonably safe.

From that starting point, it seems realistic to accept that some of the attitudes and behaviours that we have put into place to deal with our young lives (coping strategies), although perhaps necessary and useful in the moment, are not the most appropriate ways of functioning long-term.

Someone that has had to learn to be very self sufficient at a young age can find themselves being excessively independent – overly protecting their own physical, emotion and psychological spaces to the extent that they find it almost impossible to trust others and to open up to them.

On the other hand, a child that has noticed that an anxious parent is always available to solve any and all problems can well grow up to be dependant in any variety of ways.

It is only in some extreme cases that these psychological and behavioural patterns become exaggerated, rigidified and outmoded to the point that they are pathological, which we call mental illness.

However, many, (most?) of us carry with us, to a much lesser degree, beliefs and behaviours, patterns and 'positions', attitudes and actions that serve us poorly in our personal and professional lives, it is for this reason that we undertake personal work, (self-help, therapy, etc.) to change some of these attitudes, behaviours and/or reactions. If you are bothering to read this book, it is likely that you have some areas of your life that are not functioning as you might wish. (Unless of course you are a practitioner in a helping profession but then again…)

2.4 Different 'methods' or different views of the same mechanisms?

These four 'methods' I in no way consider to be mutually exclusive; quite the opposite, they are often interlinked, overlapping and even, is some ways, the same things. They are sometimes more differentiated by the particular points of view, theoretical schools and personal vocabularies of the authors, than by major differences in their functioning or effects.

For instance, when Klaas Tuinman talks of roles, he also adds that the '… information describes personality types, traits, behaviour patterns and coping strategies,' and that they '… are "normal" survival responses & strategies that become personality traits.'

And Pearlin and Schooler (Pearlin and Schooler, 1978), when describing coping, reflect that: 'Coping, in sum, is certainly not a uni-dimensional behaviour. It functions at a number of levels and is attained by a plethora of behaviours, cognitions, and perceptions' (pp 7–8.)

The reason that I have chosen to talk of all 'four methods' is to cover as many visions of the world as possible, but be they Attitudes, Behaviours, Coping Strategies or Defensive Roles, all can be dealt with and our lives improved.

As Klaas Tuinman puts it: 'They are not diseases, nor are they signs of mental illness. They are behaviours which have outlived their usefulness and now become barriers to living productive and satisfying lives. They can be changed – it is no more difficult to change them and begin living positively, than it is to hang onto them and live negatively.'

3. Stories

3.1   The use of stories for therapy, personal and profession development

3.1.1   The different types of stories used in therapeutic work

There seem to be five different types of 'stories' that are used in therapeutic work which fit into two distinct categories;

Real life stories:
-        case studies
-        personal and family anecdotes

Metaphoric stories:
-        tales – classic stories written by authors in the past
-        psychotherapeutic stories written by either a therapist himself for a certain person or family or written with or purely by the patient or family
        and finally

-        hypnotic inductions

3.1.2   The benefits of using real life stories - Personal anecdotes and case studies:

By citing real stories from our lives and those of our other patients (suitably modified to protect their identities), we offer our patients more possibility to relate to and with these stories. The fact that these are 'real' adds a dimension that other forms of teaching and stories cannot add.

Jack Haley (Haley, 1967), mentions how 'Dr Milton Erickson uses examples from his life with his children when discussing hypnosis and therapy'

Sidney Rosen (Rosen, 1982), also quotes many instances where Erickson uses the stories of his own family and of his other patients within his therapies.

On a totally different level, taking for example the highly successful 'Chicken Soup for the Soul' book series, we find that the real stories of peoples' experiences are offered as inspirations and models for the reader which then supports and encourages him in his own life.

If one looks at the contributors section of the 'Chicken Soup for the Soul' website (Canfield & Hansen, 2008), we find the following directives for potential future writers: 'We owe most of our success to writers like you for the wonderful contributions of inspiration, hope, overcoming life's challenges and realised dreams.

'... A Chicken Soup for the Soul story is an inspirational, true story about ordinary people doing extraordinary things. It is a story that opens the heart and rekindles the spirit. It is a simple, inter-denominational, living art piece that touches the soul of the readers *and helps them discover basic principles they can use in their own lives*. They are personal and often filled with emotion and drama.' (Present author's italics.)

3.1.3   The limitations of using real stories

Although real stories are easier to relate to and to model from, their limitations are that they are too specific and the message can be too direct.

Why are being specific and direct limitations?

Every good therapist knows that every client/patient comes to them with the desire to 'change without changing', that they have an inner conflict between the parts of themselves that believe that their behaviour/attitude/belief/relationship style is to some degree self-destructive and the parts that feel that it is wrong/inappropriate/impossible to change it.

These inner conflicts exist in all of us; they are normal and to a large degree healthy. However, those parts of us that resist change, the person's defensive resistances, can be activated and re-enforced when faced with clear, specific, direct messages to change.

This process is well known in psychiatry and psychotherapy, as can been seen in (for instance) the works on *Change, 'Motivational interviewing' and Le Combat thérapeutique* (Walzerwick et al., 1974; Miller & Rollnick, 2002; Salem, 2006.)

In their book, 'Motivational Interviewing: Preparing People for Change' (Miller & Rollnick, 2002), William Miller and Stephen Rollnick talk of the dilemma of change. 'Feeling two ways about something or someone is a common enough experience …

This phenomenon of ambivalence is often prominent in psychological difficulties. A person suffering from agoraphobia, for example, may say, "I want go out, but I'm terrified that 1 will lose control." So, too, a person who is socially isolated, unhappy, and depressed may express ambivalence: "I want to be with people and make closer friendships, but I don't feel like an attractive or worthwhile person." With certain problems, the part played by ambivalence is even more central. A person who is having an extra-marital affair vacillates between spouse and lover in an intensely emotional ambivalence. A compulsive hand-washer or checker may desperately want to avoid going through this disabling ritual time and time again, yet may feel driven to it by fear. Such approach-avoidance conflict is characteristic of addictive behaviours' (p. 13.)

3.1.4   The benefits of using metaphoric stories
Classic tales, psychotherapeutic creations, hypnotic inductions

Metaphors *avoid* the activity of the patients' defence mechanisms.

Nossrat Peseschkian, the founder of 'Trans-cultural Psychotherapy', who uses 'classic' oriental tales to 'open up the vision of the patient to new ways to look at life', writes in the forward of his book (Peseschkian, 1982):

'Stories that can be used as a mediator between therapist and patient are an important help. They give the patient a basis for identification, and at the same time are a protection for him...Without attacking the patient or his concepts and value directly, we suggest a change of position...'

Michel Kérouac (Kérouac, 1989) reflects that: 'The objective of the allegory is to attract the conscious attention of the individual and to inhibit his defence mechanisms so as to allow him to enter into contact with the forces of his unconscious, rich in possibilities and solutions' (present author's translation.)

Within his 'axioms of communication' (Watzlawick et al., 1967), Walzerwick states, '2.34 - *Every communication has a content and a relationship aspect...* ' (p. 54, Walzerwick's italics.)   One could continue from there in reflecting that all communication has a digital / direct / verbal / information-based / logical / left-brain component and an analogical / indirect / non-verbal and para-verbal/experiential / relationship -based/right-brain component.

The metaphor is an analogical message, delivered through a digital channel.

Using metaphoric stories bypasses the level of consciousness which reacts by creating arguments, rationalisations and reasons why change is not an option.

The metaphor is the language of the unconscious, hence it facilitates a direct communication to the unconscious.

Thus, metaphors offer alternatives within the choice of coping strategies; solutions which would normally be immediately rejected if presented directly can find a place for deeper reflection when presented indirectly.

3.1.5   Why use longer, more complex stories?

Many psychotherapists, coaches, teachers, hypnotherapists, etc. use metaphoric stories and there are many very good books on the market that offer these professionals a large selection of these stories and explanations of when and how to use them.

For the most part these stories are short, if not very short. They contain a single narrative thread, dealing with a limited time frame with little or no attempt to elaborate a story with fleshed-out characters with their own histories that explain why they act as they do and how they come to be in the situations that they are in.

Longer, richer, more complex stories serve a wide variety of purposes:

-First, their length allows the readers to have more time to disengage from their normal environment and helps re-create that *dissociative* state that we seek to invoke in our hypnotherapeutic work and to some degree it (re)creates the therapeutic framework.

-The length and the complexity also helps to distract the conscious mind and often they partly mask the metaphors so that they are less obvious, as in many of the shorter, simpler stories where the messages are so clearly stated that the use of the metaphor is all but negated. (In fact, as David Gordon, in his very complete and technical book (Gordon, 2002), states: 'There is no need that the client knows explicitly and/or consciously the pertinence of the metaphor as...all the connections and changes necessary will happen on the unconscious level.' (Present author's translation from the French)

-       Also, for some patients, the lack of logical and explicitly explained reasons for how and why the protagonists come to be where they are and acting as they do, sets into motion a series of questions or worse, a growing irritation, distracting the person from focusing on 'losing themselves' in the content of the story being shared.

-       Finally, as good story-tellers have known and used since the advent of this art, enriching the narrative with multi-sensorial associations (tastes, sights, smells, etc.) helps draw the listener deeper and deeper into the experience being recounted.

This liberal referencing of the senses and sensorial anchors is part of the most basic techniques for hypnotic inductions.

Interestingly, in their directives for future writers, Canfield & Hansen (Canfield & Hansen, 2008) describe their stories in the following terms: 'They are filled with vivid images created by using the five senses. In some stories, the readers feel that they are actually in the scene with the people.' (www.chickensoup.com)

****

4   References Part 2:

Causey, D. L., & Dubow, E. F. (1993). *Negotiating the transition to junior high school: The contributions of coping strategies and perceptions of the school environment.* Prevention in Human Services, 10, 59-81.

Dombeck, Mark (Ph.D.) and Wells-Moran, Jolyn (Ph.D.) *Coping Strategies and Defense Mechanisms: Basic and Intermediate Defenses Psychological Self-Tools* - Online Self-Help Book Copyright © CenterSite, LLC, 1995-2008

Edgette, John H and Janet Sasson. *The Handbook of hypnotic phenomena in psychotherapy.* Brunner/Mazel Inc., 1995, New York, New York.

Gordon, David. *Contes et métaphores thérapeutiques.* InterEditions, Paris 2002.
« …. Il n'y aucun *besoin* que le client connaisse explicitement et/ou consciemment la pertinence de la métaphore puisque, si la métaphore est réellement isomorphe, toutes les connexions et changements nécessaires vont se produire au niveau inconscient. » (**Ch. 6 : De quelles façons utiliser les métaphores.)**

Haley, Jay. Taken from *Advanced Techniques of Hypnosis and Therapy: Selected Papers of Miton H. Erickson, M.D.* Grune and Statton Publishers, New York, 1967.

Ingerman Sandra. *Soul Retrieval, Mending the Fragmented Self,* HarperCollins, New York, 1991

Kérouac, M. *Les métaphores, contes thérapeutiques*, Sherbrooke, Les Editions de IIIe millénaire, 1989.
« L'objectif de l'allégorie est d'attirer l'attention consciente de l'individu et de déjouer ses mécanismes de défense afin de lui permettre d'entrer en contact avec les forces de son inconscient, riches de possibilités et de solutions » (p.2)

Miller, William R. & Rollnick Stephen.
Motivationalinterviewing : preparing people for change.
2nd ed. The Guilford Press, New York, 2002.

Parker, Alison E.; Thompson, Julie A. and Halberstadt, Amy G. *Parents' emotion-related reactions and children's coping with everyday peer stressors.* North Carolina State University, May 2006.

Pearlin, L. I . & Schooler, C. *The structure of coping.* J. Health Soc. Behavior 19:2-21, 1978.

Peseschkian, Nossrat. *The Merchant and the Parrot. Oriental Stories as tools in psychotherapy.* Vantage Press, Inc., New York, 1982

Repetti, R. L.; McGrath, E. P., & Ishikawa, S. S. *Daily stress and coping in childhood and adolescence.* In A. J. Goreczny & M. Hersen (Eds). *Handbook of pediatric and adolescent health psychology.* (pp. 343-360). Needham Heights, MA: Allyn & Bacon, 1999.

Rosen, Sydney & Erickson, Milton H., *My voice will go with you, [the teaching tales of Milton H. Erickson],* W.W. Norton & Co. Inc., New York, New York, 1982.

Salem,Gérard. *Soigner par l'hypnose* Éditions Masson 2789 Issy les Moulineaux cedex 9, 2006.

Salem, Gérard *Le combat thérapeutique*. Armand Colin, Paris, 2006.

Skinner, Ellen A.; Edge, Kathleen; Altman, Jeffrey & Sherwood, Hayley. *Searching for the Structure of Coping: A Review and Critique of Category Systems for Classifying Ways of Coping* Psychological Bulletin Copyright 2003 by the American Psychological Association, Inc. 2003, Vol. 129, No. 2, pp 216–269.

Tuinman, Klaas (M.A). Dawn Cove Abbey. Deerfield, Nova Scotia 2008. e-mail: outreach@dawncoveabbey.org.

Tuinman M.A. *'Roles - Inner Child'*, www.dawncoveabbey.org , 2008.

Watzlawick, Paul, (Ph.D.); Beavin Bavelas, Janet, (Ph.D.) & Jackson, Don D. (M.D.) *Pragmatics of human communication.* W.W. Norton & Co. Inc., New York, N.Y., 1967

Watzlawick, Paul, (Ph.D.), Weakland, John, (Ch.E.), Fisch, Richard, (M.D.) *Change.* W.W. Norton & Co. Inc., New York, N.Y., 1974.

Canfield, Jack & Hansen, Mark Victor. *Chicken Soup for the Soul.* (www.chickensoup.com),

5.   Stories and associated themes

Story	1	2	3	4	5	6	7	8	9	10	11	12	13	14	15	16
Gen relaxation	I					I								I		
Tension release	I					I								I		
Contractions (Preg)														I		
Pain (muscular)														I		
Openning/Sharing Emotions	I						I	I	I		I			I	I	
Vs Anxiety	I	I			I	I		I	I	I	I	I		I	I	I
Sleep	I															
Inner Resources (Having)	I	I	I	I	I			I				I	I			
Controlling Anger						I										
Tiredness/Re-energising	I							I				I				I
Trust	I	I	I	I	I			I	I	I		I	I	I	I	I
Transformation			I	I	I	I	I	I	I	I	I	I	I	I		
Addictions	I							I		I	I			I		
Childhood lacks		I		I				I	I	I		I	I	I		
Anorexia								I				I	I			
Bulimia/Hyperphalgia	I							I						I		
Being happy	I		I					I	I	I	I			I	I	
Blocked Immaturity		I						I	I		I	I	I			
Self Love		I						I		I				I		
Self Worth			I	I	I			I						I		
Inner Resources (Using)	I	I		I	I								I			I
Self Image			I	I								I	I		I	I
Isolation	I	I	I		I			I	I			I	I	I		
Depression	I	I	I		I	I		I	I	I	I	I		I		I

By the same author

And finally

Gentle reader, thank you for downloading this book and I very much hope that you have enjoyed it.

If so, please help others to make the choice to read this by sharing your views with your friends and writing a review on Amazon.

http://www.amazon.com/dp/B00W2SHB5A

If you have any other feedback, please feel free to leave a comment on my FB page.

https://www.facebook.com/gary.gedall

Thank you,

Kindest regards

Gary

Island of Serenity Book 1
The Island of Survival

Pierre-Alain James 'Faron' Ferguson is about to commit suicide, in his suicide note he attempts to understand how he has come to have wrecked not only his own life, but also all of those around him.

Pierre-Alain James 'Faron' Ferguson finds himself in a type of 'no-mans-land', between here and there, he must accept to visit the 7 islands before he will be allowed to continue on to his next steps. The islands are named; Survival, Pleasure, Esteem, Love, Expression, Insight and lastly, the Island of Serenity

The Early Years:
Pierre-Alain James 'Faron' Ferguson is born into a well-to-do household of a factory owner, Scottish father and mother of a noble French.

He, and his younger brother Jay, grow up in a home of two distant but invested parents. Already, the first, small stones of his future problems are being put into place.

The Island of Survival:
Faron finds himself on the first of the seven islands, transformed into a prehistoric human form, he must learn how to interact with the local environment and the early humanoid tribe.

Here, he must reconnect with his instinct of survival.

Island of Serenity Book 2
Sun & Rain

This is the second chapter of Faron's life history, in which he falls in love, becomes a real cowboy, starts boarding school, finds his two best friends, and more than that would be telling too much.

FREE: If you have not yet read Book 1, Survival, no worries, I have included a shortened version, so as to introduce you to the story and the main characters.

Island of Serenity Book 3 (Vol 1)
The Island of Pleasure
Parts 1 & 2

Part 1.

Faron finds himself in a past version of Venice, as the owner of an old but grand hotel that doubles as the meeting place for the wealthy men of the City and the high class escort girls that live in the establishment.

Faron can do anything that he likes without limitation or cost. Not only can he avail himself of the girls, but can eat and drink, without limit, but never suffer from a hangover, nor gain a gram.

So why has the enigmatic guide brought him here, and will his limitless access to life's offerings really bring him the pleasure that he is destined to experience?

Part 2.

Faron is transformed into an adolescent tom boy. In this more modern version of Venice, 'he' has just 7 days to be made into a high class escort girl. What does this experience and the intrigues of the other persons within his sphere, mean for him, on his continuing quest to understand, and to experience, Pleasure?

Island of Serenity Book 3 (Vol 2) The Island of Pleasure
Parts 3 & 4

Part 3.

Faron finds himself in the mystery of a long ago China.

Who is this sad, young man that he must help to find back his pleasure in life?

And how does he end up in the middle of a war that it is impossible for him to participate in?

Part 4.

Faron arrives in India; projected into past moments of a native, and profoundly experiencing the realities of the present, Faron finally integrates the concept of pleasure into his tortured soul.

Tasty Bites

(Series – published or in preproduction)

Face to Face   A young teacher asks to befriend an older colleague on Face Book, "I have a very delicate situation, for which I would appreciate your advice"

Free 2 Luv   The e-mail exchanges between; RichBitch, SecretLover, the mother, the bestie, and the lawyer, expose a complicated and surprising story

Heresy   An e-mail from a future controlled by the major pharmaceutical companies, "please do what you can to change this situation, now, before it happens …

Love you to death	A toy town parable, populated by your favourite playthings, about the dangerous game of dependency and co-dependency
Master of all Masters	In an ancient land, the disciples argue about who is the Master of all Masters. The solution is to create a competition
Pandora's Box	If you had a magic box, into which you could bury all your negative thoughts and feelings, wouldn't that be wonderful?
Shame of a family	Being born different can be a heavy burden to bear. Especially for the family
The Noble Princess	If you were just a humble Saxon, would you be good enough to marry a noble Norman Princess?

The Ugly Barren Fruit Tree	A weird foreign tree that bears no fruit, in an apple orchard. What value can it possibly have?
The Woman of my Dreams	What would you do, if the woman that you fell in love with in your dream, suddenly appears in real life?

None Fiction:

The Zen approach to Low Impact Training and Sports
A simple method for achieving a healthy body and a healthy mind

Many of us approach our fitness and sports activities in an aggressive and competitive fashion.

And even if we feel that we succeed to break out of our comfort zones and win against ourselves or our opponent, there is an important cost to bear.

This level of violence that we have come to accept, so as to reach our goals is also an aggression against ourselves. By removing this need to 'win at any price', and tuning in with our bodies and emotions, we can achieve an enormous amount, all the while being in harmony with our mind, body and spirit.

The Zen approach to Low Impact Training and Sports, is a new softer approach where you can have the best of all worlds.

Adventures with the Master

Dhargey was a sickly child or so his parents treated him.
He was too weak to join the army or work in the fields or even join the monastery as a normal trainee monk.

To explain to the 'Young Master' why he should be accepted into the order with a lightened program, he was forced to accompany the revered old man a little ways up the mountain.

As his parents watched him leave; somewhere they felt that they would never see their sickly, fragile boy ever again, somewhere they were totally right.

He was a happy, healthy seven year old until he witnessed the riders, dressed in red and black, destroying his village and murdering his parents; the trauma cut deep into his psyche.

Only the chance meeting with a wandering monk could set him back onto the road towards health and serenity.

Through meditation, initiations, stories, taming wild horses, becoming a monkey, mastering the staff and the sword; the future 'Young Master' prepares to face his greatest demon.

Two men, two journeys, one goal.

The Tales of
Peter the Pixie

Peter the innocent, honest, young pixie, and his friends; Elli, the, 'much older then she looks', modest but powerful Fairy, Timothy, the old, trustworthy, Toad and the, ever so noble, Fire Dragon, are the best of friends.

Together, they experience many wonderful and heart-warming adventures.

Told in a classical children's story style; Peter and his friends, meet all kinds of creatures and situations.

As with all children, Peter is often confronted with experiences that he does not know how best to deal with, and he often reacts in ways that are not the most appropriate. Fortunately; with the help of his good friends, good will and common sense, everything always turns out for the best.

Picturing the Mind

A simple, single model, accessible to everyone, to explain the development, functioning and dis-functioning of the human psyche.

Abstract:

For the common man and woman in the street, the complex and competing theories and models of the human psyche; its development, functioning and dis-functioning are often unhelpful for their understanding of themselves.

This becomes even more problematic when they find themselves in difficulty, as often, even the mental health professionals, who are experts in their own fields, find themselves at a loss to communicate successfully how and why the patent is unwell and what needs to happen to find or regain a healthy balance.

This opens up the question; 'is it possible to image a simple, single model, accessible to everyone, to explain the development, functioning and dis-functioning of the human psyche?'

One that builds on existing theories and models, benefitting from the mass of experience and research of 'modern western' psychological concepts and ideas, but also integrating traditional visions of the human psyche and modern theories from the physical sciences.

Picturing the Mind, is an attempt to answer to this need.